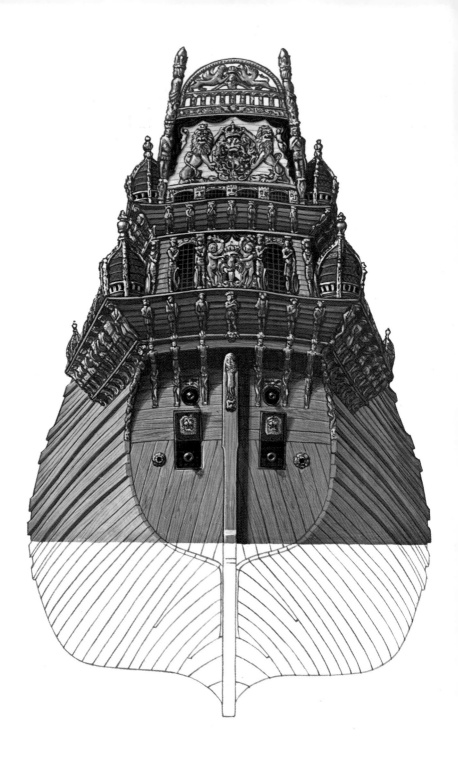

The stern of the Royal Ship Vasa

Sailing Ships

in words and pictures
from papyrus boats to
full-riggers
by

Björn Landström

Doubleday & Company, Inc.
Garden City, New York

First published in 1969
Reprinted and re-issued in larger format 1978
Produced by
Interpublishing AB, Taptogatan 4, S-115 28 Stockholm
© 1969 Björn Landström
All rights reserved
Library of Congress Catalog Card
number 72−83811
ISBN 0-385-14408-3

Printed in Spain by
Printer industria gráfica sa, Tuset, 19
Barcelona, Sant Vicenç dels Horts, 1978
D. L. B. 17732-1978

Preface

Readers in various parts of the world have been asking for a concise edition of my book "THE SHIP", which was published in 1961. New and important finds have been made since that time, and as I have also learned a great deal that is new, from my own researches and those of others, I decided that the best thing to do was to revise my previous book thoroughly, and to add certain entirely new sections. The subject is an enormous one and it has not been difficult to find material for this book, which at the same time supplements and corrects my previous work.

To limit its scope, and to be able to work with the things I best understand, I have restricted myself to sailing ships, and sailing ships only from the western world, including the Mediterranean countries. Even so, of course, this book is still only a general survey, a gallery of types. Up to the beginning of the 17th century, the material available is often both inadequate and ambiguous, and for this reason I have included also the original representations on which my reconstructions are based. For the sake of clarity, however, the former are often presented as line drawings, based on photographs. From the beginning of the 17th century, the material is sufficiently rich and clear for the inclusion of such sources to be unnecessary.

In collecting my material and in many of my reconstructions, I have relied largely on the authors whose works are quoted in the List of Sources. I have also been in direct contact with the following research workers, with whom I have had rewarding discussions: Doctor Moh. H. Abd-ur-rahman, Cairo, R. C. Anderson, Litt. D., Fordingbridge, England, Doctor J. van Beylen, Antwerp, Commodore G. A. Cox, Amsterdam, Rear Admiral Julio F. Guillen, Madrid, Lars-Åke Kvarning, Stockholm, B. W. C. Lap, Rotterdam, Per Lundström, Stockholm, Commander José Martinez, Barcelona, Doctor Ahmad Youssof Moustafa, Cairo, Commodore Antonio Namorado, Lisbon, Doctor J. B. van Overeem, Rotterdam, Baron G. B. Rubin de Cervin, Venice, Doctor Anvar Shukri, Cairo, Professor Vivi Täckholm, Cairo, and Gösta Webe, Stockholm. To all these people, I should like to express my warmest thanks.

Björn Landström

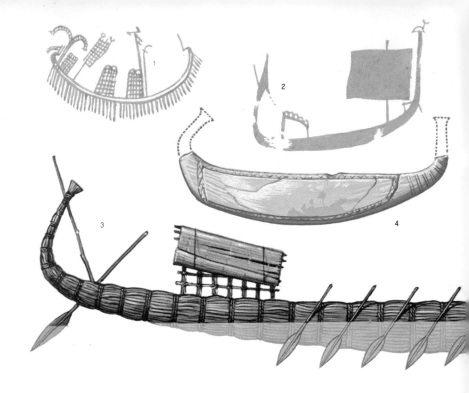

Egyptian ships

We do not know when man first began to build boats or use the wind as motive power, but the oldest unmistakable pictures of sailing craft come from Egypt. The Nile was the ideal area for the emergence of primitive shipping. Papyrus provided the material for rafts, which were early on made spool-shaped and given turned-up ends. The wind in Egypt is northerly practically all year round, and it was only natural that people should soon hit upon the idea of exploiting it for voyages up the river, which was incomparably the most important route for traffic.

The earliest known picture of a sailing craft (1) is to be found on a vase made in about 3200 B.C. Another picture of a sailing craft (2), also painted on a vase, is probably a hundred years younger. Both hulls are shaped like papyrus rafts (reconstruction in Fig. 3). No good ship's timber has ever grown in Egypt, and even down to our own day it has been customary to build smaller craft at least of short, rough planks of acacia and sycamore. The earliest certain representation of a built wooden boat, a little model carved in bone (4), is from about 3000 B.C. It is shaped like a papyrus raft (i.e. it is papyriform), and assuredly had the typical

turned-up stems. The model is dug out, and the artist has marked with a zig-zag pattern the seams that in reality joined the sides to the bottom and stems.

Papyriform wooden vessels were to be built throughout the age of the Pharaohs, and they seem to have been intended exclusively for persons of distinction. Plutarch writes that the goddess Isis travelled in a papyrus boat when searching for the corpse of her husband Osiris, mentioning a general belief that persons travelling in such craft were never attacked by crocodiles. A newly made papyrus raft is green, and it was common to paint the hulls of papyriform wooden boats green, while the turned-up ends were magnificently decorated, sometimes in imitation of the binding on the stems of papyrus rafts.

Various pictures show how special covers of cloth or leather were used from early on to help shape the ends of these rafts (5), and we later on find such covers imitated on wooden craft (6).

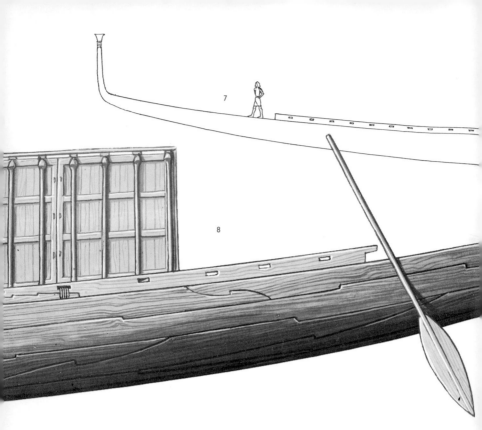

As early as around 3000 B.C., timber, above all cedarwood, was imported from the Lebanon, largely for use in shipbuilding. The oldest vessel in the world, the "boat" of Cheops, was built of cedarwood in about 2650 B.C. It was found in 1954 by the southern side of the Great Pyramid in an airtight and watertight tomb, stripped down into its simple parts like a giant building kit. Almost all its parts were excellently preserved, and only a few had been damaged by rot where the wood had been in direct contact with the rock tomb. The largest planks are 23 m. long, 52 cm. broad, and 14 cm. thick, weighing about a ton.

To make it easier to assemble the large parts, each detail was first copied on a scale of 1:10; with this smaller building kit a boat was then built which proved to be elegantly papyriform (7), 434 cm. long and 60 cm. broad. The real boat, which at the time of writing is being assembled in a museum of its own, will be 43.4 m. long and 6 m. broad.

The ends of the planks are fastened to each other by long scarfs with hooks (8). The edges of the planks also have hooks, which help to keep the long and graceful hull firm. They are joined to each other by wooden tenons, which have been hammered in and glued into the corresponding mortises (9). When the parts were lifted from the tomb, the glue on the tenons was

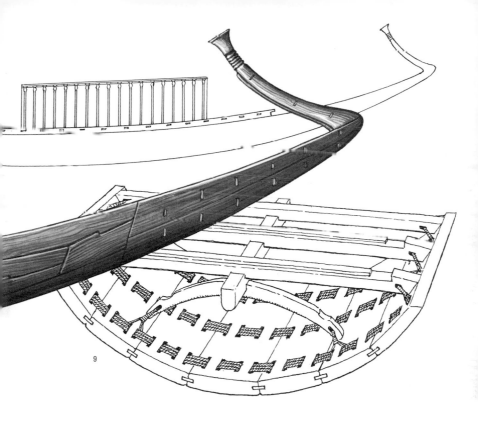

still tacky — after 4,600 years! On the inside of each plank is a
system of four rectangular mortises, breadthwise, which meet two
and two at an angle; through these run ropes, making a sort of
rib (9). The ends of the deck beams are let into the uppermost
planking, and a central shelf is borne up by a row of curved supports. The deck is laid as hatches over the deck beams. The stem
and stern consist of dug-out halves. The deck-house is 9 m. long,
and contains two cabins. Along the walls is a row of columns,
supporting an extra beam above the roof. There were fragments
of canvas in the tomb, and it is possible that the whole deck-house
was to be covered by a tent. This would give double, heat-insulating walls, a blessing in the Egyptian climate. From more recent times, we have pictures and models (see p. 22) showing gaily
patterned deck-houses. These we can see as heat-insulating tents,
decorated with appliqué.

Cheops' boat is no sailing vessel. Probably it has never floated
on the Nile, and was intended exclusively for voyages in the Pharaoh's life after death. We can be sure, however, that Cheops had
one or more similar craft also during his earthly life, and that they
were built along the same lines. From this burial craft and later
models and pictures, we can try to form some idea of all the other
big Egyptian vessels of wood.

Pharaoh Sahure, who reigned around 2500 B.C., sent ships both to Punt in East Africa and to Syria, and sea-going ships (10) were found portrayed in his burial temple. A small model from the same period (11), flat-bottomed and with angular bilges, have the same characteristic stems and sterns, and it is not impossible that the sea-going hulls were shaped in the same way. To reinforce them fore-and-aft, a number of ropes were stretched over fork-shaped supports from bow to stern, and made taut with the aid of a stick thrust between these ropes. A double belt of rope, tautened by a thinner zig-zag rope, ran round the entire hull at deck level, and gave it further strength. We must assume that this vessel was otherwise constructed in the same way as Cheops' boat. See the reconstructed longitudinal section (12).

Bipod masts seem to have been usual at this time. When the ship was under oars, the mast was dropped and rested in a tackle. Possibly, stones were attached to the legs of the mast so that it could be more easily raised. The positioning of the mast well forward permitted sailing only if the wind was well astern. The sail was tall and narrow, and was possibly controlled also by a lower yard. The vessel was steered by six rudders, three on either side.

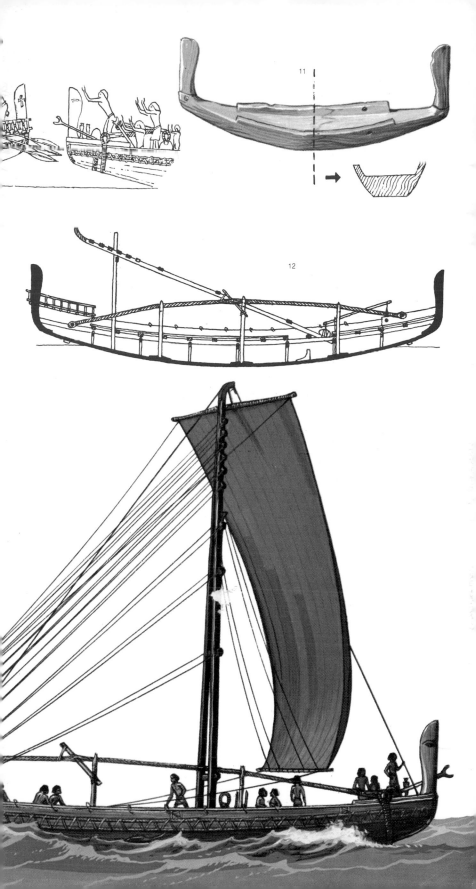

11

12

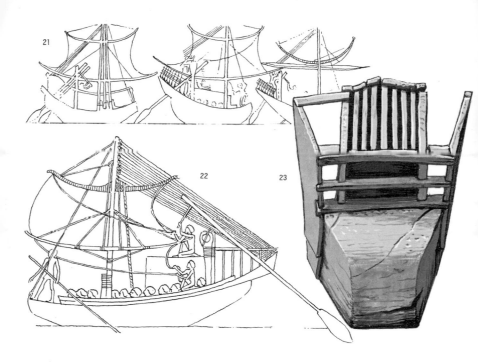

A wealth of source material is available in the form of paintings, reliefs and models of Nile craft from the period 2500—2300 B.C. The models show that most vessels were flat-bottomed, with angular bilges (17, 19, 20, 23), even if occasional round-bottomed models have been preserved (18). Single masts, bipod masts, and even tripod masts (21) occurred throughout the period, but it seems that masts were gradually shortened and sails were instead made broader towards the 24th century B.C., when the system with many rudders was also abandoned in favour of only one or two rudders (21, 22). The positioning of the mast far forward, with a single forestay and many stays aft, shows that sails were used only with a following wind. Some pictures show members of the crew sitting on the lower yard to keep the sail taut in a good breeze (14). Later the lower yard was fixed to the mast with guys (22). The sail was manipulated with braces from the upper yard and sheets from the lower.

Pure cargo vessels (15, 19) had a sort of pen amidships for the cargo, sometimes also a deck-house forward and always a large deck-house in the stern. When travelling down river the mast was always dropped (15), and the crew punted and rowed to give the craft steerage-way. Up river there was a following wind, and it was possible to raise the mast (16) and set sail. Notice how the Egyptians portrayed bipod and tripod masts as if the legs were placed fore-and-aft in the ship (10, 14, 16, 21), while common-sense and a model (17) say that they were athwartships.

The above reconstruction is based on a relief in the tomb of a courtier called Ipis (22), and a model from that of Queen Neit (20, 23). Both the upper and the lower yard were held up by lifts, possibly so that the lower yard should not dip into the water if the

14

ship was rolling. The plan (24) shows how some of the deck hatches could be removed to make room for the oarsmen, who sat and rowed on the deck beams. The collapsible mast is supported at deck level by a strong knee.

15

The years 2280—2052 have left but few traces in Egypt, but the period 2052—1778 is all the richer in finds. From this time we have numerous models of Nile craft, both papyriform (30) and round-bottomed, almost spoon-shaped (26). We do not, however, have any models of vessels used exclusively for cargo.

Apart from the papyriform craft, which were always steered with two rudders, vessels now have a single, very large rudder that rests on the curved stern and is supported by a strong pole. A remarkable detail is the "bowsprit" (26, 29), possibly the support for a forward steering oar (32) that could be useful travelling down river. The mast was single, collapsible, and supported at deck level by three knees (26, 27). The lower yard was suspended from a large number of lifts. A painting shows a greatly reduced sail (28), and since we find, on a model, a sail divided into two (30), we venture to believe that bonnets were used even at this time, long strips which were lashed to the foot of the sail and could easily be removed to reduce the sail area. We have no pictures of sea-going craft from this period.

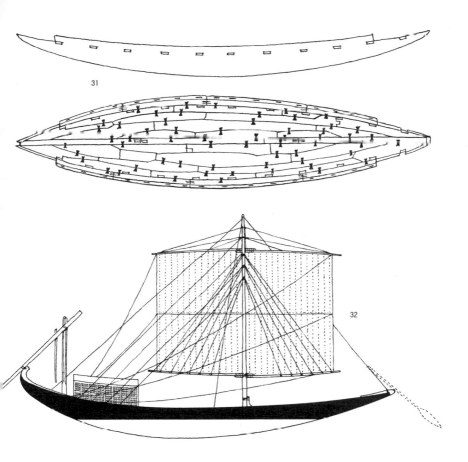

31

32

On the other hand, boats have been found built of short planks (31). They are about 10 m. long and 2.3 m. broad. The 8 cm. thick planks are joined together with tenons and with hourglass-shaped pieces of wood, the ends of which fit into adjacent blocks. The reconstruction (32) shows the probable proportions of one of the larger Nile craft.

Below is a model with a large deck-house. We must imagine this frame to be covered by a tent.

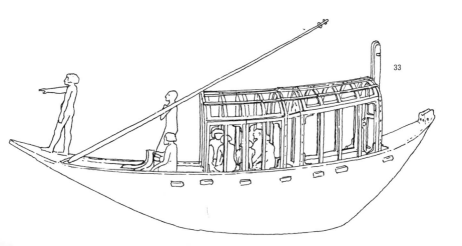

33

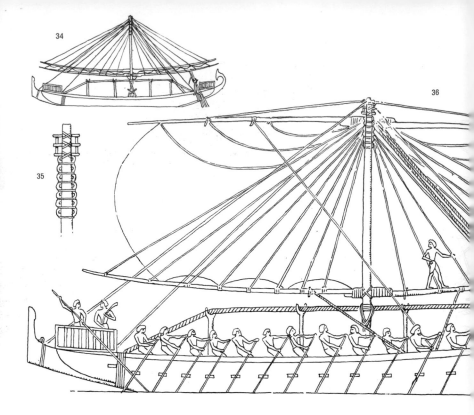

After another period of decline lasting around 210 years, Egypt flourished during the years 1567—1085. Apart from the boat of Cheops, we do not have a richer or more clearly interpretable material relating to ships from any other early age. Our most important source, perhaps, are the reliefs of sea-going ships that Queen Hatshepsut caused to be made around 1500 in her burial temple in Deir el-Bahari. These show, among other things, five sailing ships on their way to the land of Punt, which perhaps lay in Somaliland, perhaps as far down as Zanzibar. They show also five ships, with sails lowered, loading incense, myrrh and other precious goods. These pictures are very fine and rich in detail (34, 36), and the man who originally drew them knew both ships and his trade. But like all other Egyptian artists he let his ships float far too high in the water. — We have also good models from roughly the same period, which supply supplementary details (37, 38), and there is little room left for guesswork.

For the first time, we encounter ships with keels. It is uncertain whether ribs had begun to be used to support the planking, or whether ropes were still used as in the time of Cheops (see p. 9). The deck beams protrude in a long line through the side, and they were surely locked between the planks so as to give the necessary

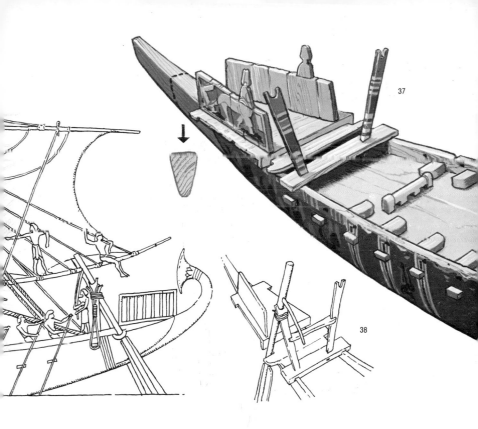

strength athwartships (cf. the belt of ropes, p. 10). In spite of the powerful keel, the hull was still supported by a hawser from stem to stern. This was stretched downwards by a twisted rope close to the mast. In those days, as now, it was common on Nile boats for the oarsmen to sit on the deck beams and make room for their legs by lifting away hatches in the deck (cf. pp. 14 and 23). Some models, however, show short benches for the oarsmen (37), and it is probable that such benches existed also on the Punt ships. The mast-block typical of the time can be seen in a detail (35). Through the uppermost holes on either side of the masthead ran the lifts, and through the next holes the thick double halyard. Through the three uppermost of the round holes ran the lifts of the upper yard, through the four lowermost the lifts of the lower yard. The mast still has no shrouds, but two forestays. A stay aft and the double halyard support the mast in a following wind. The positioning of the mast amidships suggests that the ship could be sailed in half-wind, and possibly a point or two into the wind, at least with the help of the oars. Notice that the sailing Punt ship is rowed at the same time. Previous sources show ships either under sail alone, or under the oars.

A reconstruction of a Punt ship is shown overleaf.

19

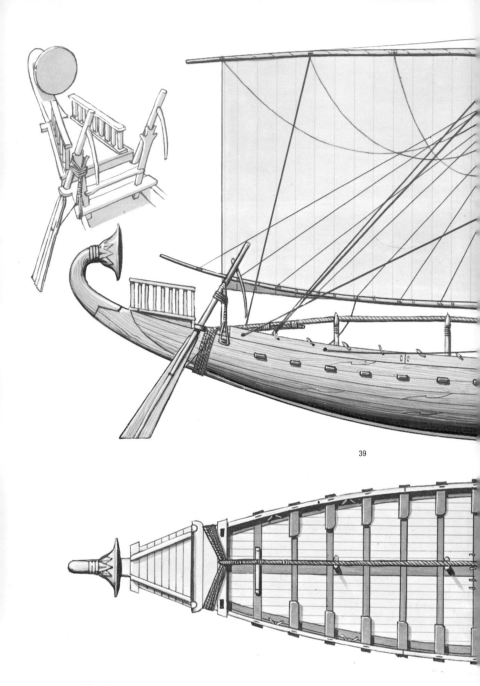

39

The Punt ships show fifteen oarsmen on either side, and I have assumed in reconstruction that the distance between oars was 2 Egyptian cubits, i.e. 105 cm. The length of the hull is then about 25 m. The beam is, at an estimate, around 5 m., the draught perhaps 1.3 m., the sail area 130 sq.m. We can say that the hull is semi-papyriform, and the stern-post ends in a stylized papyrus flower.

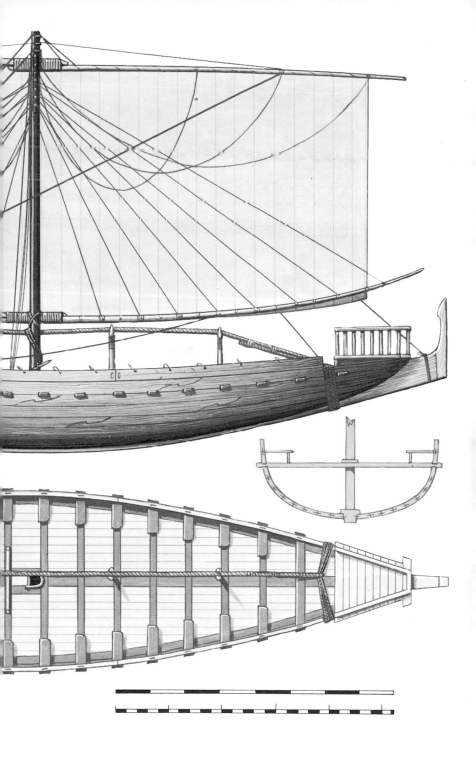

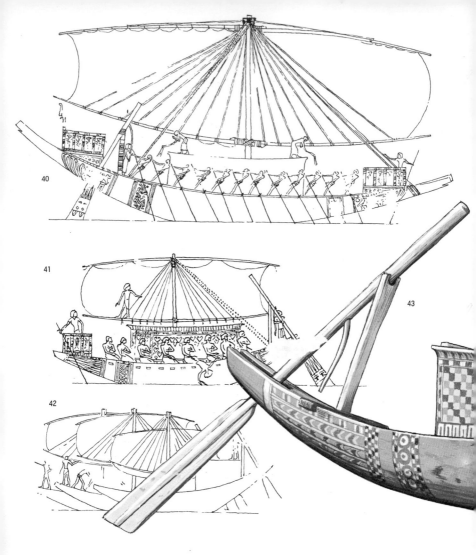

40

41

43

42

We have numerous pictures and models of luxury craft for travel on the Nile dating from the 15th and 14th centuries (40, 41, 43). All these have a large cabin amidships, which was perhaps covered by a tent (cf. Cheops' boat, pp. 8—9). The largest Nile craft seem to be shaped mainly like the Punt ships, with powerful prows extending far beyond the rabbet (40). The rigging and stays are the same, and although the pictures are not always clear the models show (37, 38, p. 19) that two rudders were used. Smaller craft and cargo vessels (41, 42), however, have an almost spoon-shaped hull, in which the one rudder rests in a recess in the stern-post, and is supported by a pole (43).

About 1200 B.C., Egypt was threatened by a large invasion force. The inscriptions call the enemy "the people from the sea", and they were probably tribes from Crete, the Philistines of the Bible among them, who were now forcing their way into Egypt

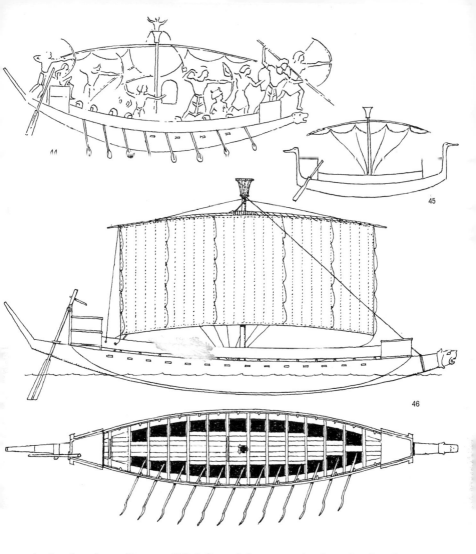

by land and sea. Ramses III defeated the enemy both on land and
at sea, and he caused his battles to be portrayed in a temple. The
pictures we find there of ships are less detailed than at Deir el-
Bahari, but we see anyway that a clear advance has been made
during the three hundred years. The Egyptian ships (44) are
equipped with rams, the invasion craft (45) have vertical stern-
posts and stem-posts. Both types have a single yard, and the sail
has been furled by drawing it towards the yard with brails. Both
types also have "tops".

It is difficult to say how large these vessels were. The invasion
craft are depicted without oars, while the Egyptian have 6—11
oars along the side. In my reconstruction of an Egyptian warship
(46), I have given it 12 oars on either side and a total length of
about 24 m. The beam is something over 4 m., the sail area 80
sq.m.

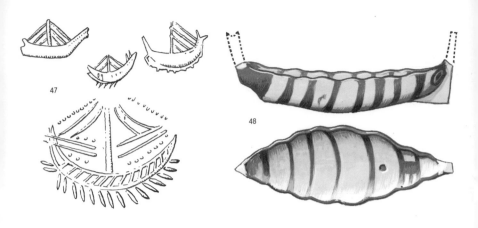

Merchant ships during the classical era

No historical period before the 17th century A.D. offers us a clearer picture of its ships than Ancient Egypt. When we turn to classical antiquity, we have usually to content ourselves with ambiguous pictures and simple models that leave all too much to the imagination.

Apart from Egypt, Crete was probably the oldest sea power in the Mediterranean, but the pictures we have of Cretan vessels from about 2000 B.C. (47) are far too schematic to give us any real idea what they were like. One of the vessels carries double yards, like contemporary Egyptian craft. It is uncertain whether the transverse stripes mark thwarts or ribs. The stern-posts of all four ships seem to be in the shape of fish-tails, and three of the ships show a protuberance, almost like a ram, on the stem-post. A small clay model (48) from the Aegean shows the same protuberance, which for want of a better term I would call a "cutwater", a prolongation of the stem which must have helped to keep the ship on course. Here there is hardly any doubt that the stripes denote ribs.

We can distinguish between two primary methods of constructing wooden vessels, a shell construction and a skeleton construction. With the former, the hull was first built up either by the Egyptian method, with the planks being fastened to each other by tenons (see pp. 8—9 and 16—17), or by the Nordic method, with the planks clinched or "clinked" to each other, and the ribs subsequently inserted for reinforcement. With the skeleton construction, the keel, stem and stern-posts, and ribs were first raised, after which the planking was added.

24

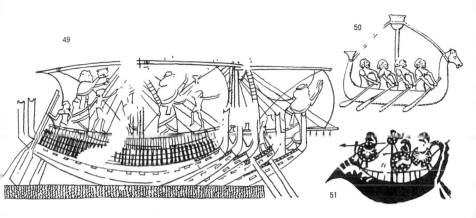

It cannot be proved, but I believe it probable that the Cretans, Phoenicians and Greeks, as the Romans demonstrably did later, built their ships on the same principles as the Egyptians, namely with the planks pegged to each other and the ribs inserted in the finished shell. We do not know when people started to build on the ribs, using the skeleton construction. It may have been well into the Middle Ages.

The Phoenicians left behind them a firm reputation of having been the most prominent trading and seafaring people of their times, but there is not much we know of their ships and the little we do know comes from Egyptian, Assyrian and Greek portrayals. Such second-hand information in the form of stereotyped pictures is of little value, and it is pointless to try to reconstruct the Phoenician ships. Phoenician trading ships (49) are portrayed in an Egyptian tomb from about 1500 B.C., and an Assyrian relief from 700 B.C. shows a ship with the prow in the form of a horse's head, which is also probably Phoenician (51). Another Phoenician vessel is to be found on an archaic vase (51). The Greeks called one type of Phoenician ship *hippoi,* horses, and another type *gauloi,* troughs or tubs. The latter suggests a round ship, a capacious trader, perhaps three times as long as it was in the beam, a basic type that was to survive in the Mediterranean until modern times.

The Egyptian pictures (49) show hulls with through-going deck beams. The vertical stern and stem-posts are cloven in the form of fish-tails. A ladder runs to the masthead, where we can sense a "top". These ships are steered with double rudders. A long fence keeps the deck cargo in place. A votive jar (?) is bound to the stem-post. We see tops and fish-tails in the two other pictures. And on the Archaic vase (51) a cutwater (or ram ?) and a fence (or storming bridge ?).

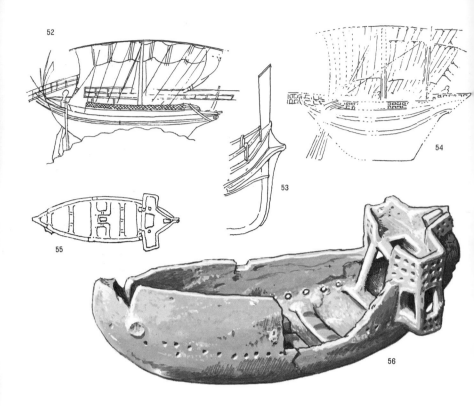

The authors of antiquity let us understand that there were many types of ship in the Mediterranean, and the few pictures we have of merchant ships from the great days of Ancient Greece confirm this. The drawings on these two pages show ships, not only Greek, from the 6th and 5th centuries B.C.

52. A small Greek trading ship, shown on a vase. It can have had a cargo capacity of 500 talents, or 13 tons. As on ships from the time of Ramses III, the sail surface is reduced by means of brails. A bridge runs from the helmsman over the deck cargo, to the bow. The gangway is fastened to the stern-post. We see here for the first time a hull with *wales,* narrow planks that are thicker than the rest of the planking, and which, together with the rails, run out aft in a sort of spray. Particularly on warships, this spray of wales and railings, the *aphlaston,* was made fairly extravagant (see pp. 44 and 49). The projecting part of the bow, with the eye, has survived — without an eye — on certain types of Mediterranean craft into our own time. — 53. The fore-post of a present-day Maltese fishing vessel. — 54. A two-masted cargo ship, drawn from an Etruscan grave painting. The dashed lines denote damaged parts. The shape of the hull is largely identical with the

26

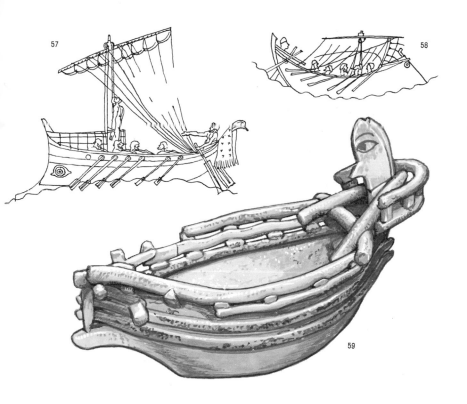

Greek ship, even if it is probably considerably larger. Both ships have two rudders, and this was to be the rule in the Mediterranean until the 14th century A.D. — 55. 56. A clay model from Cyprus, probably portraying a large round ship, perhaps one that could carry 1,000 talents, or 262 tons.

57. A trading ship, or perhaps a pirate ship, on a Grecian vase. The picture really depicts Ulysses' ship, but is modelled on some small contemporary vessel. The writers of antiquity speak of *kerkouroi,* combined traders and warships. It is possible that some trading ships were fitted with rams, so that they could combat pirates. It is also probable that the longer waterline resulting from the ram made the ship sail better. We see that the yard is raised by a double halyard running in a block on either side of the masthead. — 58. A ship with a ram (cutwater ?) on a Grecian vase. — 59. A clay model from Cyprus with the same shape of prow as 52 and 54. The sides are raised by a fence, possibly to hold together a light, bulky cargo. It is not impossible that the model, in spite of its roundness, portrays a trader-warship, and that the "fence" is in fact the outriggers for the oars (cf. p. 38).

27

60

61

The above pictures are based on the clay models on the previous page (56, 59), and show how these vessels may have looked in reality. They are Cypriot vessels from 500 B.C., but cannot have differed much from contemporary Greek ships. Greek vessels at least were usually built of pine, while the yard, joined together of two parts, and the mast were of spruce. I have already mentioned the wales, the thicker planks along the upper part of the side, but one of the models in particular (59, reconstruction 61) makes me suspect that these lists, which were called *zosteres,* or belts, lay outside the planking and had the same function as the belt of rope on Pharaoh Sahure's sea-going ship (see p. 10). Both models show a strong through-going beam slightly aft of the fore-post.

28

We find the same beam on reliefs of Roman trading vessels (63, 75), and it was to survive on Mediterranean traders into modern times. I have previously referred to it as a riding bitt, but since its true function is uncertain it seems best for the present to use the Italian name *catena*.

The planking was coated with wax or tar, or with a mixture of both. As a protection against ship-worm, the hull, underwater, was often sheathed in thin lead plating. Pictures of Greek ships show neither stays nor shrouds, but even Homer says that the mast was supported by two stays forward and one aft. The sail was usually of linen, and ropes of flax or hemp.

The above pictures are drawn from originals dating from about 50—200 A.D., and show merchantmen from Ancient Rome. The larger Roman round ship was called a *corbita,* and pictures 63, 67 and 68 must be assumed, surely, to represent corbitae. The protruding Greek "clipper bow" recurs, drawn somewhat higher up (67, 68), and ram prows also occur in a few pictures of trading vessels (62, 66). The round ship, shaped mainly as in the model from Cyprus (56), is dominant, however. On larger vessels, the stern-post often ends in a goose-neck or swan's neck. Some ships appear to be built with through-going deck beams (62, 63, 67), and in a couple of pictures we can trace a catena (67, 68). The rudders lie partly protected between the planking and a piece of the bulwark, which runs aft outside the hull proper like a pair of "wings".

The Etruscan grave painting from about 450 B.C., with its twin-masted ship (53), is unique, but we must assume that twin-masted vessels occurred before this and were perhaps quite common in the 5th century B.C. All the larger Roman vessels seem to carry two masts. The forward mast, the *artemon,* slopes forward, and the artemon sail is usually very small (68). It was presumably carried primarily to facilitate steering. A few pictures,

30

however, show an artemon with almost half the surface of the mainsail (62), and one shows an apparently small vessel with two equally large sails (64). A mosaic from Ostia shows a three-masted vessel with three sails, but this is unique.

We see that the forestay is stretched with *dead-eyes* and *lanyards,* and for the first time we find shrouds (63). These too are tautened with dead-eyes and lanyards, or some system of lanyards. The mainsail is hoisted as previously with a double halyard, and the yard is supported by lifts (65). Above the yard it was possible to set a triangular topsail (63). The brails of the mainsail run through rings on the front of the sail. The larger ships have galleries round the stern, and one of them actually has a gallery round the prow (67).

Below is a Roman wooden anchor, found in the Lago di Nemi. The arms have bronze fittings and the stock is of lead.

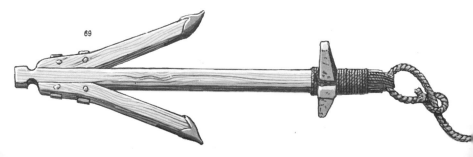

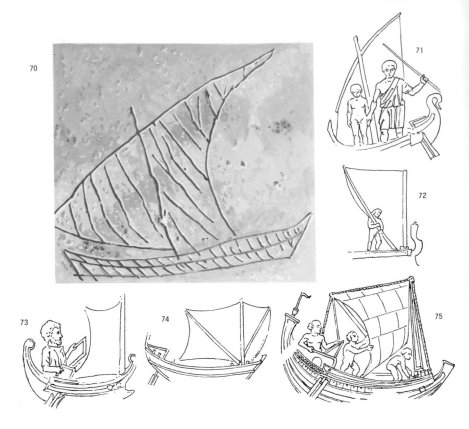

It has generally been thought that the lateen sail was introduced in the Mediterranean only in the Middle Ages. A Greek tombstone from the 3rd century A.D. admittedly shows something that could be taken as a lateen sail or lug sail (71), but most people have preferred to interpret it as an ordinary square sail sheeted home for sailing to windward. However, there was recently found on Thasos in the northern Aegean an amphora with a carving that undoubtedly showed a ship with a lateen sail (70). With this, we must assume that the lateen sail existed also during the classical period, at least in Greek waters.

It has also been believed that the fore-and-aft spritsail was first introduced towards the end of the Middle Ages; recent evidence shows that it was used by both the Greeks and Romans. A relief from Thasos, dated to the 2nd century B.C., shows the fore body of a ship with a fore-and-aft spritsail (72). Two reliefs (73, 74), one of which shows a ship running with double spritsails, have been found in the Dardanelles. This suggests that also the fore-and-aft spritsail originated in the northern Aegean, or possibly the Black Sea. That it was later used also in the western Medi-

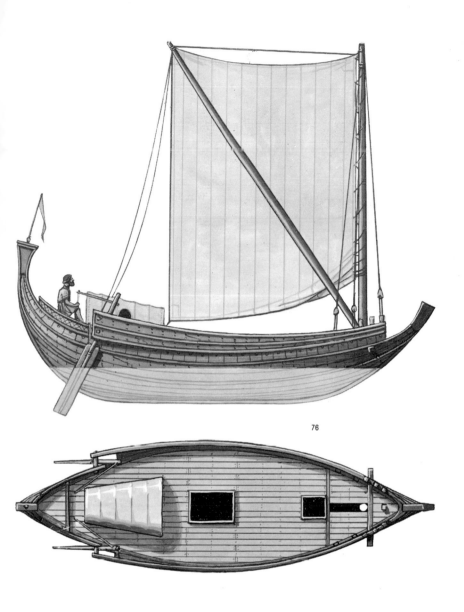

76

terranean is shown by a picture on a Roman sarcophagus from the 3rd century A.D. (75).

The reconstruction (76) shows a small Roman coaster with a fore-and-aft spritsail. The hull is shaped mainly like a corbita. The mast is immediately aft of the catena, and the halyard serves also as a forestay. Notice the three bitts in a row on each side. We can see them in the original (75) and also in a relief of a large ship (63). These three bitts in a row recur in pictures of Mediterranean ships into the 13th century. This ship might have been 12 m. long, and 3.5 m. in the beam. The sail area was perhaps 40 sq.m.

33

77

Reconstruction of a corbita from the 3rd century, according to a relief found in Ostia (63). The usual cargo capacity was 10,000 *modii,* or 86 tons. The length can have been 25 m., and the beam 6.5 m. Mainsail about 140 sq.m., topsails together about 30 sq.m.,

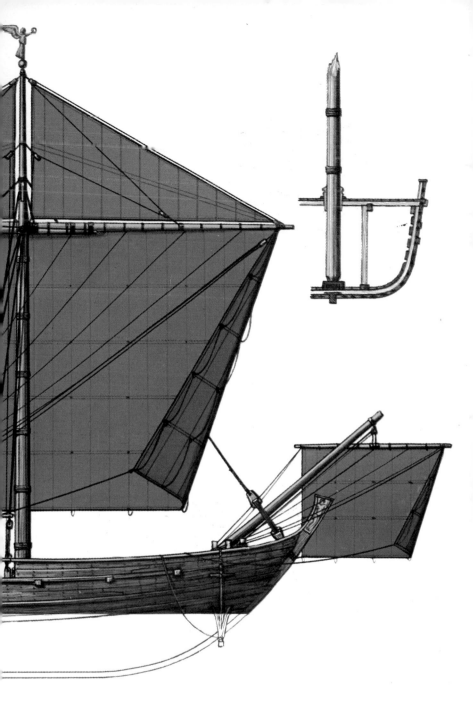

and artemon about 17 sq.m. The rudders could be hoisted from the water with lanyards when required; this was done, for instance, when the ship was running before a gale, as described in St. Luke's account of St. Paul's journey to Rome.

35

Warships during the classical era

The earliest pictures of ships from the Mediterranean countries apart from Egypt come from Syra, one of the Cyclades. They have been dated to 2800 B.C. (78). They have what can be interpreted as a ram, and a high stern-post. A slightly later little model from Crete (79) gives us an idea of their appearance. We cannot say whether they were paddled or rowed. If these craft, as I believe, were dug-outs, then there was only room for one oarsman on each bench, unless the oars rested on an outrigger.

Not until 1,500 years later do we find vessels depicted that are clearly designed for war (80, 81, 82). These are painted on pottery of the Doric Age, and have the shape of sharp-nosed, horned monsters. The shape of the ram convinces me that the hulls were dug-outs. These craft were obviously rowed (82), and one of the pictures (81) shows with all desirable clarity an outrigger for the oars. In the more complicated pictures, the artist has been concerned to show both that there was some sort of fighting bridge (80) and that the oarsmen sat two and two on each thwart (82). Not above each other, as some have believed. Perspective was unknown in those days.

Biremes — galleys with the oars placed on two levels, or in groups of two — are to be encountered first in Assyrian reliefs from the 8th century B.C. (83, 84). These are believed to portray Phoenician warships. Here too I believe that the actual hulls were dug-out trunks. In one of these reliefs (84), we see that the arms

36

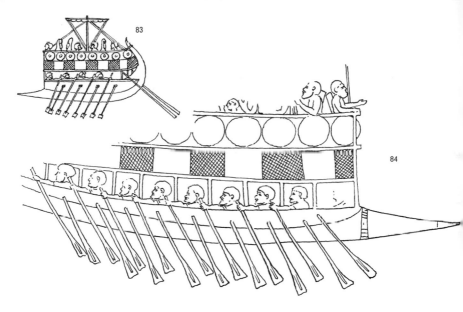

of the outer oarsmen are lying outside the supports bearing the long fighting bridge. We can interpret this as meaning that the outriggers, which supported the oars, were fitted with planking, and that the outer row of oarsmen sat outside the hull proper, over the outriggers. The vessel was slim, and easily propelled, and the outriggers gave it greater stability when it heeled over. Warriors could move about on the narrow fighting bridge without jeopardising the balance of the ship.

Overleaf are shown reconstructions of both the Doric and Phoenician warship. I see the latter as a direct development of the former. Possibly, as happened later in other parts of the world, the sides of the hull were heated and pressed out to make it broader, and additional planks may have been added to raise the freeboard. Basically, these craft were still "dug-outs". — Below, by way of comparison, the prow of a canoe still in existence in the Bismarck archipelago.

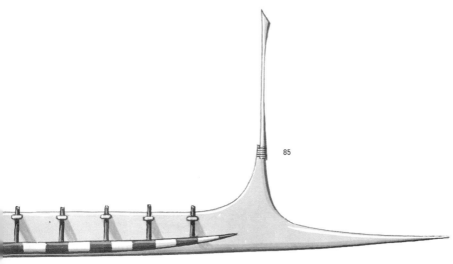

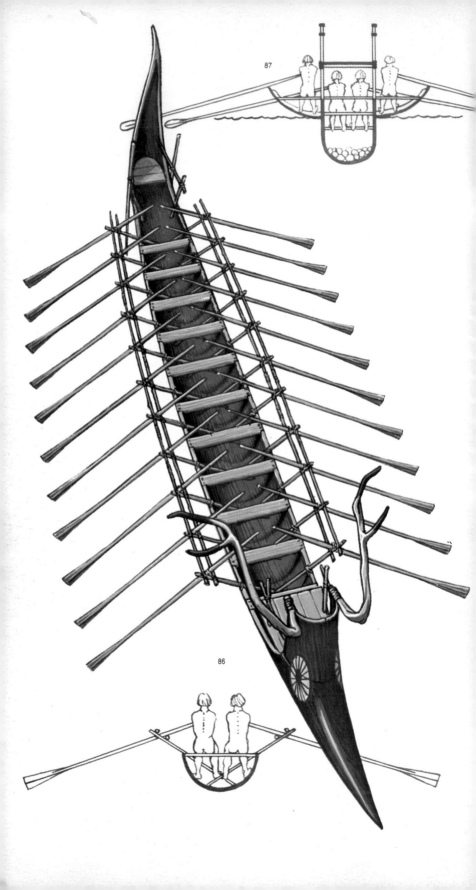

87

86

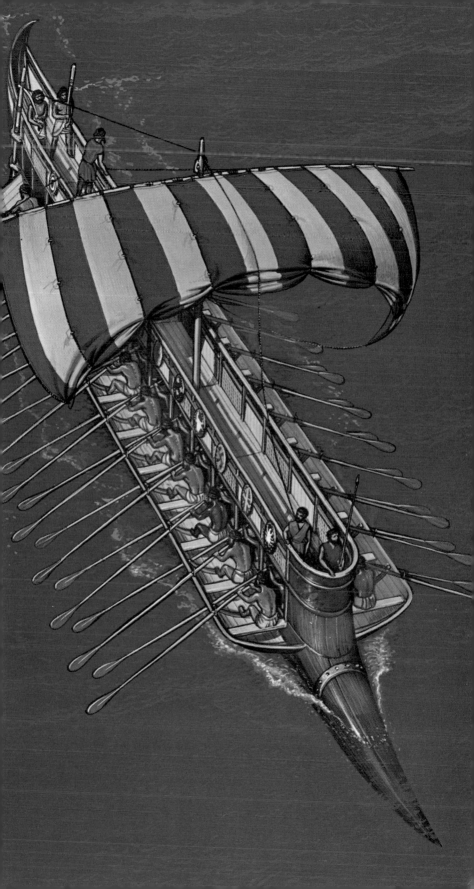

88

89

90

91

The pictures of Greek warships we encounter on vases and dishes from the 6th century B.C. are the lightest and most elegant craft we know of from classical times (88, 89, 90). They are definitely *built,* i.e. planked and ribbed. We know that they were so light that the crew, if necessary, could haul them on shore for the night, presumably, of course, stern first.

The keel was the backbone of the ship, and the storming bridge running from stem to stern gave further reinforcement (see reconstruction, 91). It seems as if the stem-post rose at the forward end of the fighting bridge (88, 90), and it is possible that the ram itself was not an integral part of the construction of the keel, but only nailed on so that it could be torn loose after a powerful ramming without too much harm being done to the ship.

One picture (89) shows the oars resting directly on the rail. The outrigger, however, makes me think that the boat is a bireme, and that only the lower bank of oars is shown. Another (90) shows some oars passing through round holes in the side of the vessel and others resting on the outrigger. The length of the hull in the reconstruction (91) is determined by the number of oarsmen, fifty in all. As they sat at different levels and at different distances from the rail, the seats could be placed closely together. The length, ram included, could have been 24 m., and the beam 3 m.

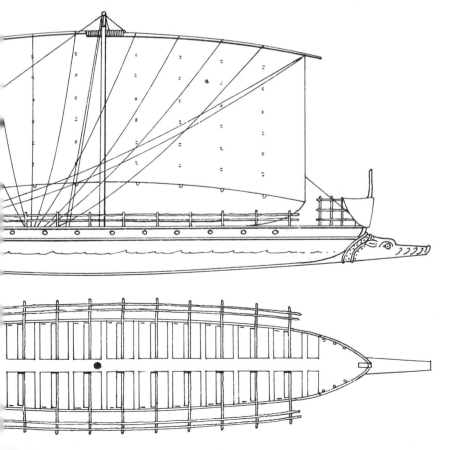

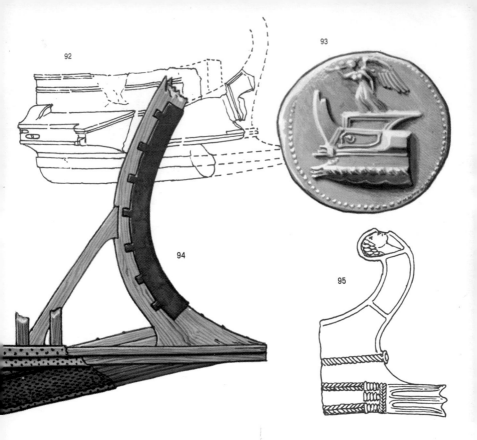

The most important and most frequently mentioned warship during the great age of Greece was the *trireme,* in which the oars lay at three levels or in groups of three. The trireme has been the most heatedly discussed of all vessels among modern scholars. A fair amount of material is available in both literature and art, but it is highly ambiguous and we do not possess a single complete picture of a Greek trireme.

When the triremes of the Athenians were not in use, they were pulled up on the ship-sheds of the dockyard in the Piraeus, and from the measurements of these ship-sheds we know that the trireme was at most 41 m. long and something under 6 m. broad. It was rowed by 170 men. The 62 outermost oarsmen were called *thranites.* 54 oarsmen nearest to the centre-line of the trireme were called *zygites,* and 54 who sat furthest down in the ship were called *thalamites.* The oars of the thranites and zygites were 9 cubits and 1 finger long, i.e. 4.47 m. We know that the oars of the thalamites were shorter.

The trireme had two rudders, two gangplanks, three boathooks. The mainmast was lowered before battle. There was one heavier and one lighter sail. Before 330 B.C. there was also a foresail, on a forward mast. Two leather tarpaulins, one on either side, pro-

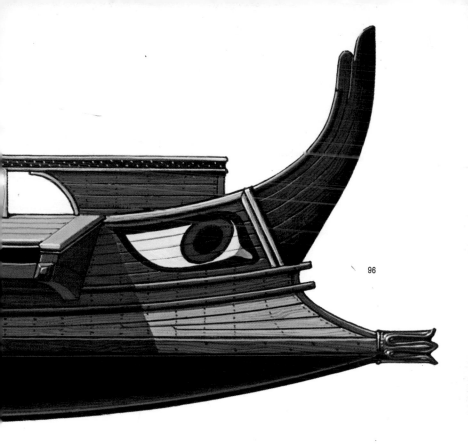

96

tected the oarsmen. For ceremonial purposes there were corresponding covers of white cloth. These could be rolled up on the rails. The lowest bank of oars, manned by the thalamites, had leather holsters which stopped the water from coming in through the large oar openings. Finally, there were four girdles of rope, altogether 330 m. long.

Much of the pictorial material we shall be studying to get an idea of the trireme's construction and appearance is not Greek. The Romans also had triremes, and they have left behind more pictures. Some of the Greek pictures may in fact not portray triremes, but they show in any case large warships from the period of the triremes. The pictures of prows on these two pages show: 92. Pedestal to the statue of the Winged Victory of Samothrace, in the Louvre, Paris. 4th century B.C. It is uncertain whether this is a bireme or a trireme. Note the two oval holes in the outrigger. The dashed lines indicate how the damaged parts may have looked. — 93. A Macedonian coin from about 300 B.C. — 94. The prow of one of the ships salvaged in 1932 from the Lago di Nemi, near Rome. 2nd century A.D. — 95. Roman bronze relief. — 96. My reconstruction of the forepart of a Greek bireme, c. 300 B.C.

43

97

98

99

100

101

A relief from the Acropolis showing part of the side of a trireme (97) has been interpreted by some scholars as a full-scale drawing. We know that the Greeks called the distance between the row-locks the "double figures", and we believe this distance to have been two Greek cubits, i.e. 96 cm. A number of other proportions have been worked out from this measurement, and the relief. In my opinion, however, such a reconstruction makes the trireme far too high (102), so that the oarsmen cannot have achieved an adequate effect. The oarsmen shown on the relief are thranites, and we see that their oars are resting against row-locks in the "fence" of the outrigger. The oars of the zygites emerge under the outrigger, and those of the thalamites between the wales. In the picture, I have marked one group of oars more clearly. The other oblique lines below the outrigger we can interpret as supports for the latter. Other pictures of Greek warships (98, 99) shows that the supports between the thranites are curved inwards in order to carry a roof over the oarsmen, i.e. a fighting bridge.

A carving on a Grecian bronze vessel (98) and a Grecian vase painting (99) show the stern of a warship. At least the latter seems to be a trireme. Where the gangway rests on the outrigger, we see a thole-pin. The black holes below the outrigger are for the oars of the zygites, and a hole below these is intended for the aftermost thalamite oar. The outrigger is supported by both S-shaped and straight supports, and the fighting bridge by S-shaped supports.

A relief on Rhodes shows the stern of a warship (100), which seems to agree with the pedestal of the Winged Victory (92). The spray of lists, the aphlaston, is highly stylized. The hoisted port rudder has its fittings in the outrigger. Below the rudder is clearly seen a girdle of ropes. On the fighting bridge is the chair of the trierarch, or commander.

A Roman trireme is to be seen on a relief from Praeneste (101). Two warriors are standing on the outrigger, on the passageway outside the thranites that the Greeks called a *parodos*. The thranites' oars are withdrawn, so that only the ends of the blades can be seen as a long ornamentation. The lower banks of oars are provided with holsters.

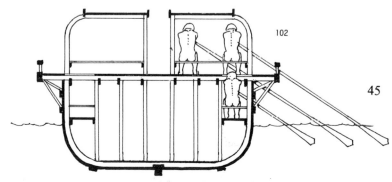

102

45

The above reconstruction is of a trireme from the 4th century B.C. A century before this, triremes were probably less compact (98, 99), the outrigger was not covered over, and the aphlaston was less stylized. The majority of scholars have conceived the oarsmen as sitting in three different banks, but I prefer to place the thranites and the zygites on the same thwarts running obli-

46

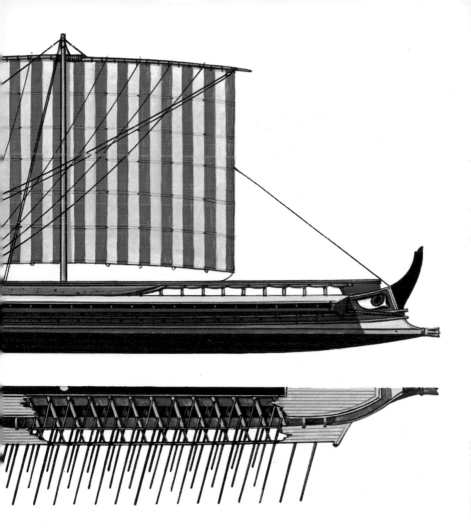

quely to the fore and aft line. We know that the thwarts of mediaeval galleys were oblique. And we know that the thalamites
sat lower down than the others. The dimensions of my trireme
are: length 41 m., beam 4 m., beam incl. outrigger 5.5 m. The
area of sail can have been 150 sq.m.

The triremes had four girdles of ropes, which helped stiffen
the elegant, lightly built hulls in rough seas and during battle.
We see parts of these girdles in numerous pictures (93, 95, 100,
103), but certain texts suggest that they ran inside the hull. In the
reconstruction, the girdle is passed around the stem-post between
the projecting wales, runs into the hull where the outrigger starts,
passes inside the ribs by the feet of the thranites (see 105 where
the belt is marked in red), and then out and round the hull close
to the rudders. The leather tarpaulin that protects the oarsmen
during battle is rolled up on the arch over the heads of the thranites (105).

47

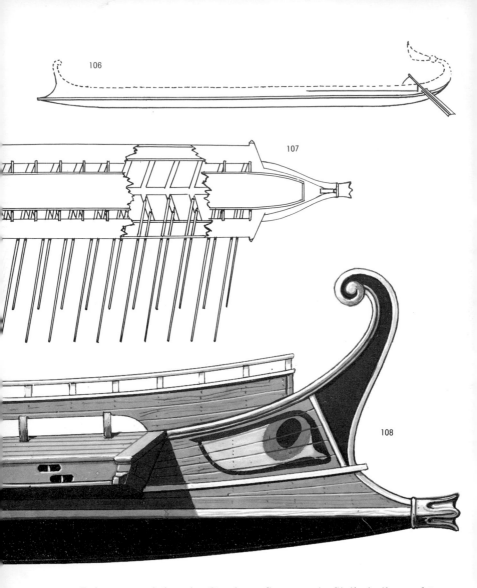

It is narrated that the Greeks at Syracuse in Sicily built *quadriremes* and *quinqueremes,* galleys with four or five banks of oars, in the 4th century B.C. We also hear of vessels with fifteen and even forty banks of oars, but we need not believe that the classical authors meant that the oarsmen sat at five, fifteen, or forty different levels. No pictures have been preserved of ships with oars in more than three banks, and I do not believe that any such vessels existed.

On the other hand, it was easy to assign more oarsmen to each oar, as long as the ships were made broad enough, and a quinquereme would then mean simply a ship with five oarsmen to each oargroup. One of the ships recovered from the Lago di Nemi (94, 106) was 71 m. long and 33 m. in beam, and this could well

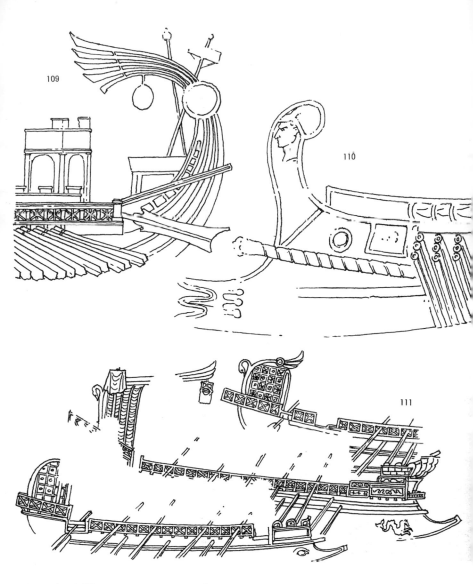

have had fifteen oarsmen to each oar.

The pedestal of the Winged Victory (92) shows a new arrangement, in which the oars of both thranites and zygites rest on the outrigger, which I interpret as meaning that the after, somewhat higher oar in the group was rowed by the zygites (reconstruction 107, 108). We have pictures of Roman biremes (109) and triremes (110), in which all the oars seem to come over the outrigger. A similar arrangement is to be found on galleys even in the late Middle Ages (see p. 112). Other pictures of Roman biremes and triremes (101, 111) seem to show the older system with the oars of the thranites over the outrigger, and those of the zygites and possibly the thalamites passing through the sides of the ship. Both systems survived into the Middle Ages.

49

112

113

The lateen sail during the Middle Ages

We have seen glimpses of the ships of classical antiquity. There were numerous different types whose name and use we know, but as to whose appearance we hardly dare speculate. Leaving classical times, we pass first through a darkness lasting six hundred years, during which we have no information on the history of the ship in the Mediterranean. Not until the 9th century do we encounter some Greek miniatures showing small craft rigged with lateen sails (112, 113, 114).

The hulls hardly differ from those of the Roman coasters (75, 76), and there seems if anything to have been a decline. When the Romans lost their dominion over the seas, voyaging became more hazardous and trade was transformed into an anxious coastal

114

115

traffic. The lateen sail was suitable precisely for coastal traffic, with a small crew, and it was more efficient than the square sail in sailing close-hauled. It is hardly probable that the square sail had vanished from the Mediterranean, but we do not find it depicted again until the 14th century.

One of the miniatures (112) shows most of the details characteristic of the lateen sail rig (reconstruction 115). The halyard always ran in a block *above* the shroud attachments. Since forestays could not be used, the mast often sloped slightly forward. The shrouds were tautened with lanyards, and could easily be thrown loose when sailing on different tacks. The long yard was bound together of two or more pieces and held to the mast by a parrel in the form of a slip-knot, which could easily be loosened from the deck. The sail was checked by two tackles to the lower yard-arm and two braces, which usually started slightly below the upper yard-arm.

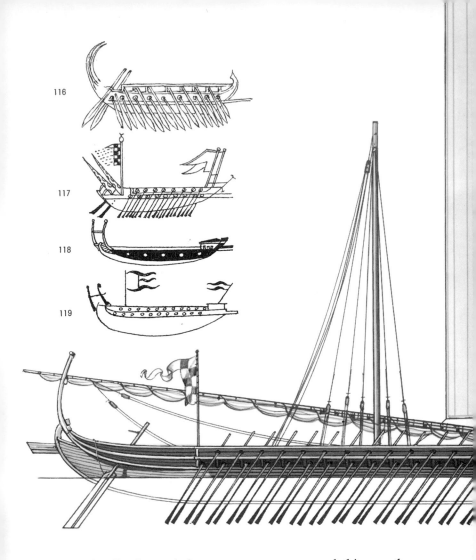

116

117

118

119

The Greek word *dromon* means runner, and this was the name given to a type of small vessel which was to be found in the mouth of the River Po in the 5th century A.D. A hundred years later we learn of Byzantine warships of the same name. Originally they were probably fast, light craft, but later on the biggest ships in the Byzantine Navy were called dromons. According to information from the early 10th century, a dromon was rowed by 200—230 men at altogether one hundred oars, in two banks. In the upper bank there were three men to an oar, in the lower only one. A somewhat smaller type with 162—164 oarsmen was called a *pamphylos*, and a type with 108—110 oarsmen an *ousiakos*. The smallest type, with oarsmen in one bank only, was called a *moneres* or *galea*. It is from the latter that we have the word galley.

We have no pictures extant of early dromons; only from the end of the 12th century and early 13th century do we have any

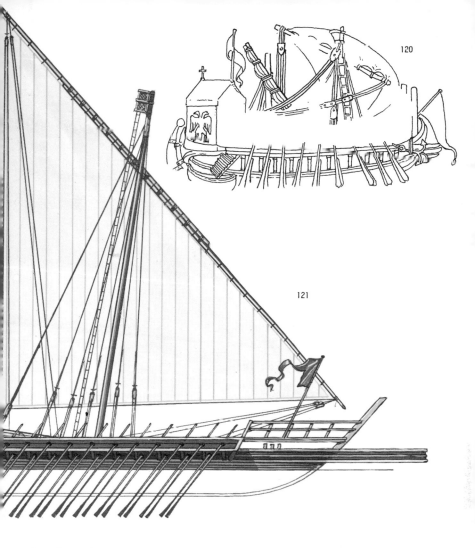

120

121

drawings that may depict Byzantine warships (116—119). Three of them show oars, or holes for oars, in two banks, and one of them (117) has something that can be seen as an outrigger. It is improbable that the dromons lacked outriggers, as some scholars have suggested, since we know that warships both previously and subsequently had them. The ram, which previously lay at the waterline, has now been raised above the water. The double struts in the stern, which we will encounter also on merchantmen of the same period (see next page), I believe to be gallows for the lowered lateen sail yard.

Another picture of a Byzantine warship, which is admittedly from about 1430, but which shows many antiquated features (120), has contributed details for a reconstruction of a dromon from the early 13th century (121).

53

122

125

123

124

The Italian republics of Genoa, Pisa and Venice, together with Marseilles and Barcelona, were in control of Christian shipping in the Mediterranean during the crusades. Pictures of merchantmen from the 13th century are admittedly naive and very stylized, but they have certain details in common that give us some idea of what these ships looked like in reality.

In the main, the proportions of the hull were apparently much the same as those of Roman trading vessels. We see that the ends curve sharply inwards, which suggests that the sides, or at least the bulwark, also curved inwards. All larger ships had some form of after-castle, and the typical crutches for the yard were

126

127

128

fitted in one way or another into the castle. In one case at least (127), these crutches appear to be a direct continuation of the bulwark, which at the stern runs outside the hull to incorporate the rudders (cf. 77). This is how I have drawn them in the reconstruction (126, 128). Two pictures show a forecastle resting on the rail and the curved stem-post as a roof over the foredeck (125, 127). The majority of larger vessels were two-masted, but we find also three-masted ships (122). The foremast, which was usually the tallest, sloped forward, and a ladder led up to the top (123, 127).

A relief in the church of San Eustorgio in Milan, unusually detailed for its time, shows a single masted merchantman of 1339 (129). Two rows of through-going beams suggest that the hull was double-decked. We see for the first time a hawse for the anchor cable, but a rope from the same hawse runs around the forepart of the ship. This could be a "girdle". The reconstruction (130) tries to give the ship its true proportions.

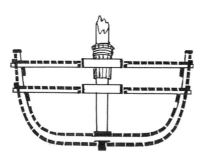

130

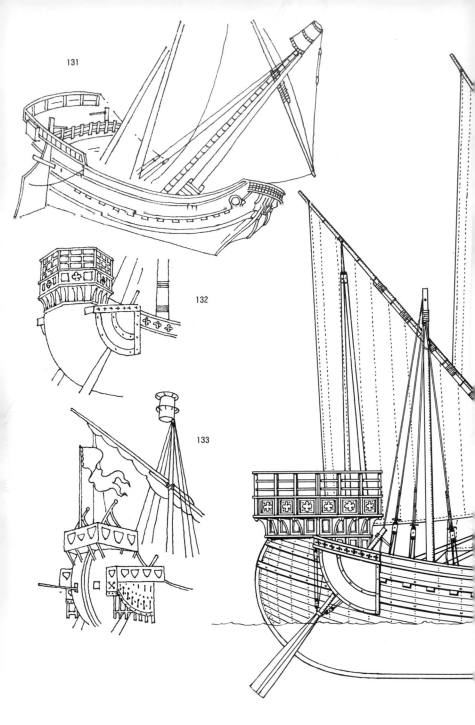

Two pictures show two sterns (132 133), in which the rudders are protected by narrow galleries and by sectors apparently sheathed in metal. A not very clear picture of a Venetian ship (131), which probably has three masts, shows through-going beams, the end of the catena, a rounded forecastle, an anchor hawse, and

134

a curving of the prow that suggests a cutwater. Since the shape of the after-castle and the rudder arrangement are not clear, I prefer to combine two of the pictures in my reconstruction of a merchantman of the 14th century.

59

135

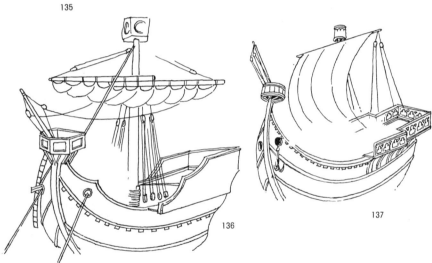

136

137

A Florentine manuscript describes how pirates from Bayonne, in France, came to the Mediterranean in 1304 in *cogs,* and how merchants in Genoa, Venice and Barcelona at once began to build similar ships. As we shall see below (pp. 76—79), the Northern European cogs were square-rigged, straight-ended and fitted with stern-rudders; we find ships of precisely this kind in a Spanish miniature from 1350 (135). Another couple of pictures of 14th century Mediterranean craft (136, 137) show square sails and castles of a type that recalls Northern Europe, and from the following century the square sail and stern-rudder appear to dominate.

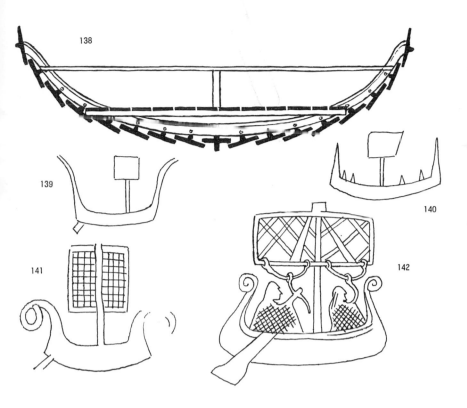

Mediaeval ships from Northern Europe

During classical times and the early Middle Ages, contacts between the Mediterranean countries and Northern Europe were only sporadic; it is probable that Northern shipbuilding developed quite independently, at least in the early stages. It is true that people have speculated as to a possible connection between the warships of the Vikings, the "drakkars", and certain Phoenician ships (cf. p. 25, Fig. 50), but the similarity is only apparent.

Nordic vessels differed from Southern European primarily in the way they were built. Northern craft were clinker-built, i.e. the edges of the planks overlap. Mediterranean craft were carvel-built, i.e. the planks meet edge to edge. The Nordic system is illustrated by a cross-section of a boat from the 7th century A.D. from Kvalsund, Norway (138).

The oldest portraits we have of Northern European sailing ships (139—142) come from the pictorial stones on Gotland, dating from the 7th and 8th centuries. These show both straight and round-ended vessels with one mast, a square sail, and often a side rudder.

61

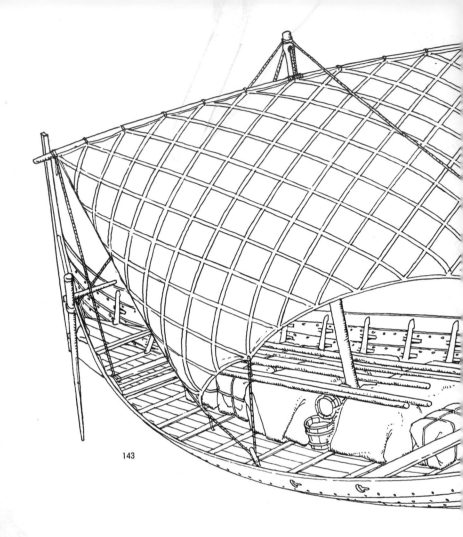

143

If we had nothing else to go on, we would think that the pictures showing the stem and stern-posts at a sharp angle to the keel (138, 139, 141) were simply badly drawn. But a 9th century wood carving found in Norway portrays the forepart of a ship (144) in an almost naturalistic way, and we see there practically the same "cutwater" as we found previously in the Mediterranean.

I believe that many sailing ships in Nordic waters, above all merchantmen, which were more dependent than warhips on good sailing qualities, were fitted with cutwaters. The majority of the more detailed pictures of ships we find on the pictorial stones show sails that are chequered, mostly on the diagonal (141, 142, 145). Sails were often made of homespun, which became weak and stretchable particularly when the sail was wet. We can therefore assume that the diagonal lines mark reinforcements in the sail, of double-thickness homespun, linen, or leather. I have pre-

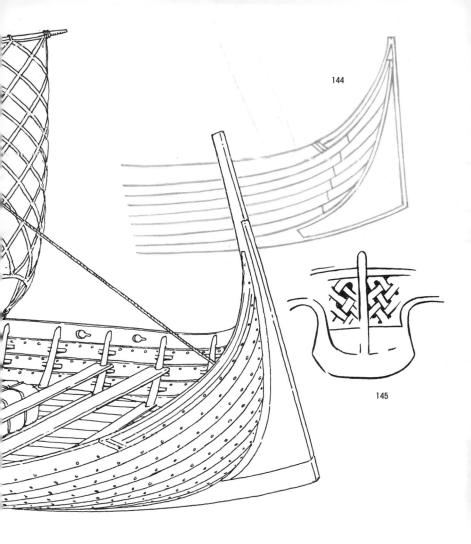

144

145

viously interpreted some of these pictures as indicating a yard also at the foot of the sail, but I am now inclined to think that there was only one yard.

The reconstruction (143) is based on the pictures shown here and on subsequent finds of ships; it tries to show what a small merchantman looked like during the 7th or 8th century. An open hull, in which the cargo lies amidships. Room for eight oarsmen — and seldom did a trading vessel actually have this large a crew. Homespun sail with leather reinforcements. And the Nordic rudder, a long oar that was usually, if not always, on the right side of the vessel, the side to which the rudder gave the name of "steer-board", or starboard. The cutwaters fore and aft increased the lateral plane of the ship, which reduced the leeway in halfwind and when going to windward. Modern copies have demonstrated their great ability to sail even to windward.

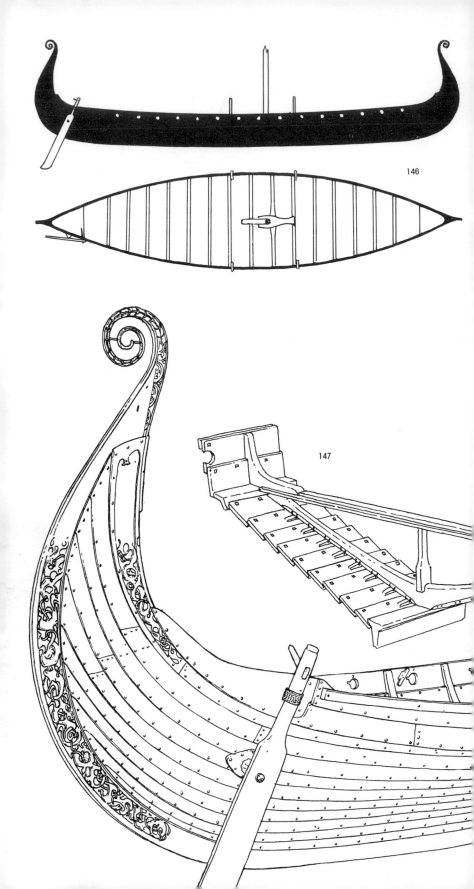

146

147

The discoveries which give us a better idea of Viking ships than any pictures and descriptions were made in 1880 at Gokstad near Sandefjord and in 1904 at Oseberg near Tönsberg, in Norway. Both vessels are well preserved, and now stand fully restored in their own museum outside Oslo. The *Gokstad ship* is dated to the 10th century, while the *Oseberg ship* appears to be a hundred years older.

The *Oseberg ship* is 21.4 m. long and 5.1 m. broad. It is built of oak, with twelve planks on either side (146—148). The ribs, which in clinker-building were always inserted only when the hull was complete, are riveted only to the ninth and tenth planks. Otherwise they are bound to cleats in the planking. The long rudder is attached to the side of the ship both by a withe that passes through the blade of the oar and a rounded block to an extra strong rib, and by a plaited leather thong on the rail.

The ship could be rowed with fifteen pairs of oars, and could also be sailed. The mast is on a stock lying directly on the keel. Over four deck beams lie the *mast partners,* open aft to facilitate raising the mast. As on Egyptian vessels, the deck is laid as hatches between the beams, and raised both fore and aft to a platform, the so-called *lyfting.* The *Oseberg ship* was no fighting vessel, however, more a pleasure craft, and in size an insignificant coaster of the sort that was called a *karv.*

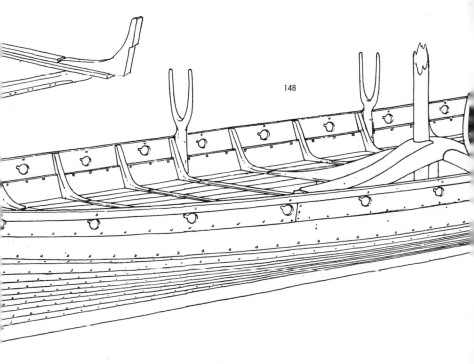

148

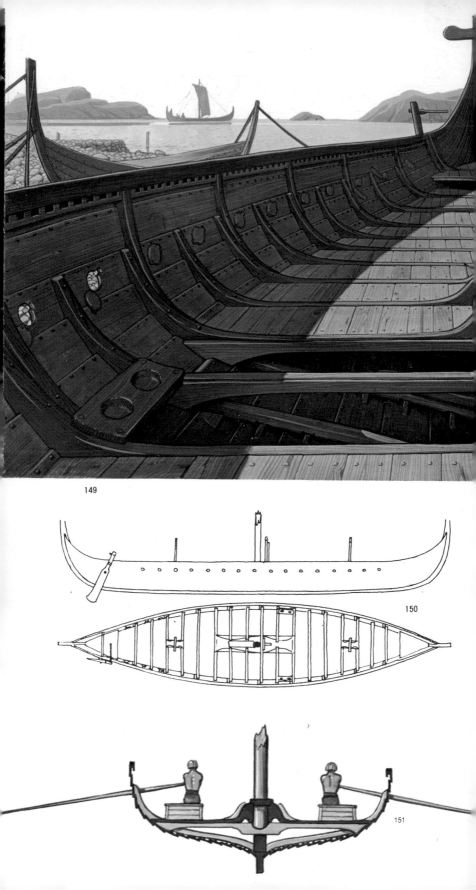

149

150

151

The *Gokstad ship* (149—151) is larger, sturdier, and more intended for sailing over open water. It is 23.3 m. long and 5.25 m. in the beam, but this vessel too is no more than a coaster, a karv. It too, is built of oak, with 16 planks on each side. The powerful *mast partners* stretch over six deck beams. Just forward of the mast close to the planking are two chocks with rounded depressions on the deck to support the *beitass,* a long pole which was set up to keep the sail's forward leech stretched when sailing close to the wind (see next page).

Neither of the two ships have thwarts for the oarsmen, and we must assume that they sat on loose benches or chests. The holes for the oars could be covered by small discs, so that the water would not gush in when the ship heeled under sail. For the *Gokstad ship* could sail and even tack.

A replica of the ship was built as early as 1893, and crossed the Atlantic in 28 days.

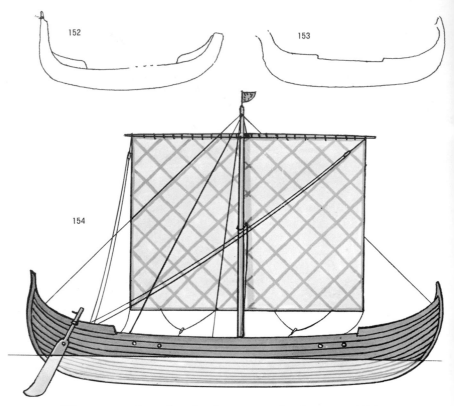

The sagas relate that the *knorr* was the foremost Viking cargo ship, but we have no descriptions or pictures of the knorr. Fighting ships were known as the "long ships", in contradistinction to cargo vessels, which must have been shorter and rounder. There certainly existed many different types of merchantmen, and subsequent development in the Baltic suggests to me that at least one type there was straight-ended, and had cutwaters fore and aft (reconstruction 155). On Swedish rune-stones we find pictures of ships with an extra plank fore and aft (152, 153), and we can believe that there existed also merchant vessels with curved stem and stern-posts of this type (reconstruction 154).

A find made at Ladby in Denmark included an anchor with about 10 m. of chain and the remains of a cable. On the *Gokstad ship* was found an anchor stock, and so we can combine the parts into a picture of a Viking anchor (157). Different blocks (156) were also found on the *Gokstad ship,* but since most of the rigging had perished the purpose of the various types is not clear.

The two reconstructions (154, 155) are as usual hypothetical, but details such as the *parrel* which holds the yard and sail to the mast, the anchor, *windlass,* and blocks are based on finds, pictures and descriptions from Viking times.

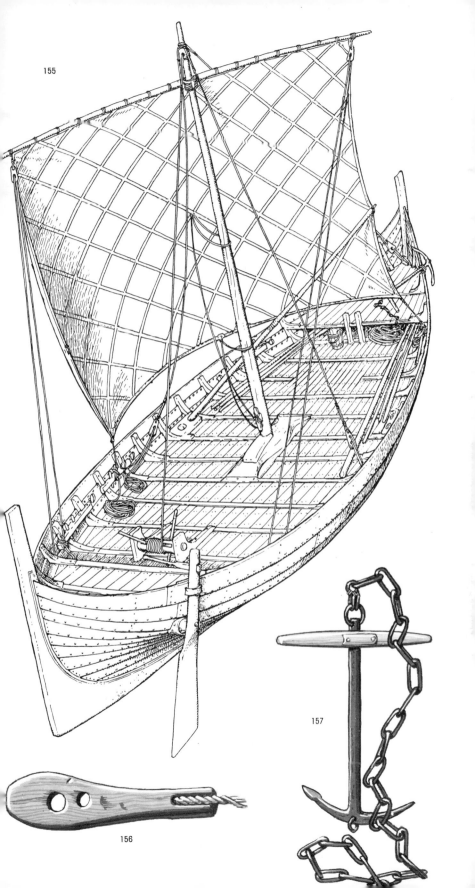

155

156

157

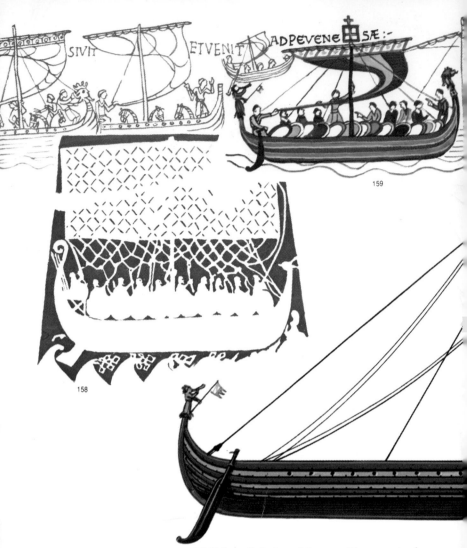

158

159

The smallest type of Viking fighting-ship would seem to have been that referred to as "*twenty-roomed*", which meant that it had twenty thwarts for rowing and forty oarsmen. 25-roomed and 30-roomed ships were also common. The ship known in Norway as a *skeid* seems often to have been 32-roomed or even larger. Like the very largest fighting-ships, it was called also a *drakkar*. *Ormen Lange,* Olav Tryggvason's famous drakkar, was 34-roomed, and Earl Håkon's ship is stated as being 40-roomed, i.e. with eighty men at eighty oars. The distance between the holes for the oars on the *Gokstad ship* is 98 cm., and the length of *Ormen Lange* can be estimated on this basis to about 46 m.

All we know of the fighting-ships comes from the literature, from Gotland pictorial stones (158), and from the Bayeux tapestry (159). A terrifying dragon's head (160) has been found in the estuary of the Scheldt, and is most certainly from a Viking

HIC EXEVNT: CABALL DE NAVIBVS

160

161

ship. We can conceive the fighting-ship as an enlarged type of *Gokstad ship,* the largest perhaps somewhat narrower in proportion. The dragon heads were detachable and were carried only on voyages of war. The Bayeux tapestry shows ships with painted sides and coloured sails. Kings' ships often had linen sails of different colours, sometimes embroidered, sometimes with applications of silk.

There are pictures from as early as the 8th century (158) showing *bowlines* running from the leeches to the stem-post, and taking the place of the beitass. We can see a raised platform in the stern, which was later to develop into a "castle", and there is also a system of sheets in bridle after bridle, designed to stretch the sail evenly. The reconstruction (161) is based on the Bayeux tapestry, and shows William the Conqueror's ship *Mora.* Observe the top at the masthead.

71

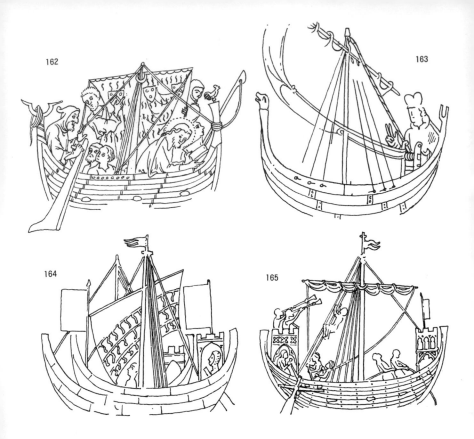

162   163   164   165

The best pictures of N. European ships after Viking times are to be found on the seals of port towns. Both these and other pictures, however, show the ships far too short and too high. The pictures on these pages are drawn from 13th century originals, and all the hulls appear to be shaped like the trading vessels of the Vikings, shorter, rounder, higher than the long ships. It is obvious that they were not rowed, since we see neither oars nor holes for oars. Since it is impossible to date the pictures exactly, I have arranged them in a logical succession.

162. A miniature of an English ship. The fork in the stern supports the mast when it is lowered. The binding around the stem provides an attachment for the stay, and at the same time probably for the *bowsprit*. The line running from the end of the bowsprit is a bowline. On the long ships, bowlines could be led directly to the stem, but shorter vessels needed a bowsprit that would carry them sufficiently far forward of the sail. This was the original function of the bowsprit. The oval objects on the side are probably cleats that protected the ends of through-going beams. On the sail we see the reef-points with which the sail was reefed.

163. A Belgian miniature shows the mastfork and a windlass for the halyard. — 164. Two ships on the seal of Hastings. We see

reef-points and an after-castle, shaped like the turret of a fortress.
— 165. The ship on the seal of Winchelsea shows through-going
beams and a long beam on the planking which supports the rudder. It has both a forecastle and after-castle. Four men are heav-
ing in the anchor cable, two of them on the windlass aft.

166. The picture on the seal of Yarmouth shows that the binding round the stem-post holds the bowsprit. The castles are built
close up by stem and stern. At the masthead is a top, built like a
castle. — 167. A miniature made in the crusader port of Acre in
Palestine shows a northern ship in which the castles appear to
be resting on the stem and stern. — 168. The castles on the ship
on the seal of Dover extend right over the ends. That the rudder
is shown on the port side is because the engraver failed to remem-
ber that the impression would be reversed. We can assume that
the rudder was always to starboard. The word *port* for the other
side was so called because it was this less fragile side that was
turned to the quay in port. — 169. On the seal of Faversham we
see a ship with a large after-castle, probably in two storeys, and a
forecastle built entirely around the stem-post. Notice the trum-
peters portrayed on practically all the seals.

73

The ship on the seal of Dover from 1305 (168) may have looked like this. Length over all about 20 m., beam 5.5 m., sail area 120 sq.m.

170

Probably some time during the 12th century, an improvement was introduced somewhere in N. Europe that was to be of enormous importance. The rudder was moved from the side to the stern-post. The earliest depiction we know of a vessel with a *stern-rudder* is a relief on the font in Winchester Cathedral (171). This is thought to be a Belgian piece from about 1180. From a few decades later we have a graffito in Fide Church on Gotland (172). In both pictures, the decoration of the stern-post seems to have been transferred to the rudder, and we see in the graffito how the tiller was taken round the high stern-post.

A type of ship directly associated with the mediaeval German trading group known as the Hansa League was the *cog*. Hansa League seals from the 13th and 14th centuries usually show straight-stemmed ships (173, 174, 175, 177), while English seals, for instance, from the same period show ships with curved stems (176). We therefore venture to believe that the cog was straight-ended, with a high freeboard, and (at least from the mid 13th century) a stern-rudder. As the stems ran straight down to the keel, the roomy, deep-draught cog had sharp ends and a long lateral plane and because of this sailed better than the shallow-draught vessels with curved stems. I see the cog as a direct successor to the Viking trading vessels with their cutwaters (cf. 143, 155).

The cog was a merchant vessel, but like, for instance, the earlier ship from Dover (168, 170), it had fighting platforms, fore and after-castles, from which pirates and other enemies were fought. During the 14th century the after-castle became larger, and in time housed the captain's cabin and accomodation for important passengers, while the forecastle shrank, perhaps so that it should not obscure the helmsman's view. The seals of Elbing and Stralsund from the mid 14th century (175, 177) show after-castles that have already begun to merge into the hull, while a drawing from the same century (178) shows the process almost complete. I do not know of a single N. European ship depicted with lifts before the end of the 15th century, and I believe that they came into use only after more intimate contacts had been established with the Mediterranean.

A ship found in Bremen in 1962 agrees in many of its details with the seals of Elbing and Stralsund, and it is thought to be a cog from the same period. This ship is 23.5 m. long, 7 m. in the beam, and could load about 130 tons. It has only twelve broad planks on each side. As on the seals, the stem-post is heavier than the stern-post and slopes rather more. The hull has five through-going beams.

The reconstructions (179, 180) show Hansa cogs from the mid 14th century. They are based on the seals of Elbing and Stralsund (175, 177), and information on the Bremer cog. I know of no picture before the end of the 15th century that shows *tack tackles,* the lines that from the clews of the square sail fixed the sail forward. However, I believe them to have existed early on, and I have included them for instance on the ship of William the Conqueror (161). On the seal of Elbing (175) we see, aft of the shrouds, an upright post, probably a sheet block, and forward of the shrouds a similar post, probably a chesstree. This is how I have interpreted them in the reconstructions.

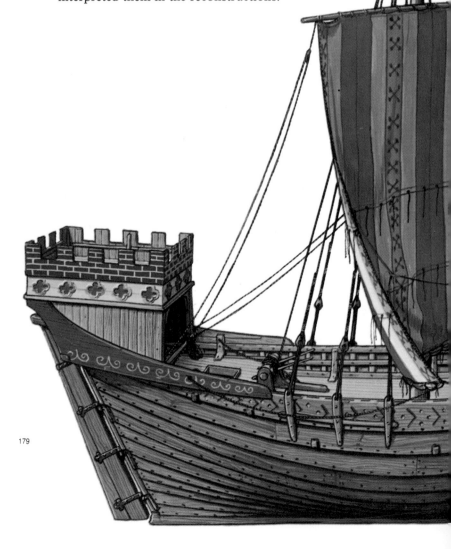

179

180

In the drained castle bay at Kalmar in Sweden were found the remains of a large number of ships, dating from the Middle Ages up to the 17th century. Best preserved was a little ship from the mid 13th century. Only its uppermost parts had been destroyed, and it has been easy to reconstruct this coaster without too much guesswork (181—183).

The hull is of course clinker-built and almost entirely made of oak. It is decked only at the fore and aft. We see altogether six through-beams, and all the cross-beams are further joined to the planking with knees. We find a windlass for the main halyard, almost exactly like that on the Belgian miniature (163). The mast, which was missing, could be lowered forward between two side supports, and locked when in the upright position by a short cross-piece fixed to the side supports with wooden pins. The ribs are riveted to the planking, no longer bound to cleats, and we can assume that the heavier ships even of the Vikings were built in this labour-saving manner.

This little craft, usually referred to as the *Kalmar boat,* was 11.2 m. long and 4.6 m. broad.

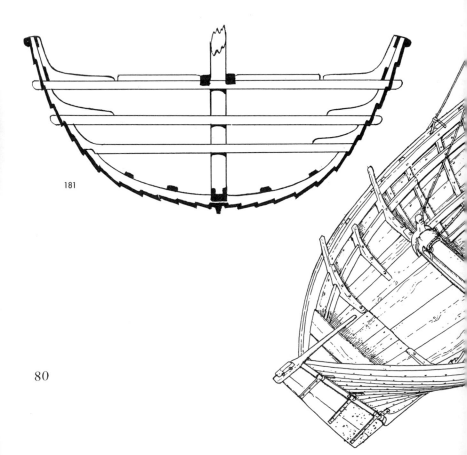

181

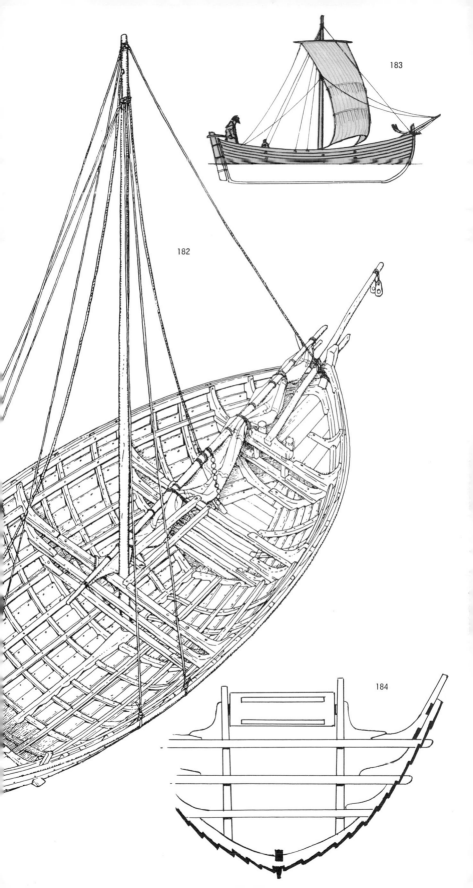

182

183

184

185. The seal of Poole from 1325 shows a ship with such a large after-castle that it may be said that the ship has a *quarter-deck*. — 186. On a painting from the end of the 14th century, at Skamstrup Church in Denmark, we see a ship that could almost be from the Viking age, with its dragon's heads fore and aft. The modern after-castle (= quarter-deck) fills the entire space aft of the mast.

187. The picture adorning the seal of the Hansa town of Danzig from 1400 surely represents the most advanced of contemporary ships. The castles are now quite a part of the hull, and the forecastle has the triangular shape that was to be common for the next 150 years. I am aware of no pictures from the Mediterranean showing the triangular castle until a couple of decades later, and I therefore believe this shape to have developed in N. Europe. It is possible that the forecastles even of the cogs were three-sided, but since we always see them straight from the side I have cautiously presented them as four-sided. Close below the castle we see a *hawse* for the anchor cable. In the Mediterrean we have found a hawse on a relief of 1339 (129). We now see for the first time *ratlines* in the shrouds leading up to the top instead of a ladder, and it was to be almost a century before these became common on southern ships. The top is also of a new type, round and with turned-out sides. We have already seen round tops on Egyptian and Phoenician vessels (46, 50), but since then they have been absent from all the representations.

188. A painting from the 15th century, at Højby Church in Denmark, still shows a ship with a dragon's head. We see the bowlines drawn in for the first time, we notice a parrel truck on the yard and a parrel in the sail at the bottom reef. A unique detail is the flagstaff on the end of the bowsprit. It will be more than a hundred years before we next see a flagstaff on the bowsprit. — 189. In a painting at Kirkehyllinge Church in Denmark we see a round-bowed ship with a hatch in the side, perhaps for loading timber or horses. It is possible that both this and the Danzig ship are *hulks*. Of the hulk we know little more than that it was capacious, and began to replace the cog towards the end of the 14th century in N. Europe.

190—191. Some ships on French miniatures from the 15th century are of much the same type as the Danzig ship. We see hooks on the yard-arms for incapacitating enemy rigging at close quarters. The lashing round the masts indicates that they were lashed together of many spars. These vessels differ from contemporary southern ships mainly by being clinker-built and having ratlines in the shrouds.

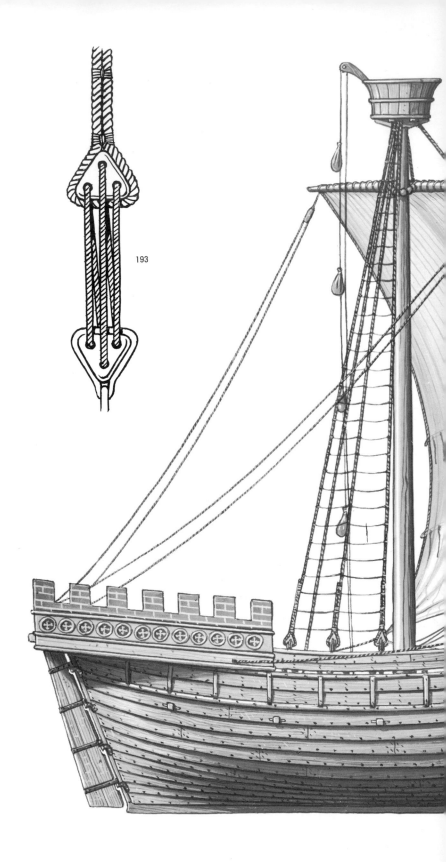

193

The ship depicted on the seal of Danzig from 1400 (cf. 187) may have looked like this. The through-beams are secured with wooden pegs, and above them we see a wale, a narrow plank that is stronger than the rest of the planking. We have seen wales on Mediterranean ships since classical times (see p. 26), but this is the first time we find them on a clinker-built vessel from N. Europe. The hoist with the bags going up to the top is for sling-stones. The shrouds are tautened with dead-eyes and lanyards in the northern manner (193).

192

Fully rigged ships

We have seen how the square sail and stern-rudder were introduced in the Mediterranean early in the 14th century (p. 60). It
had long been customary there to sail two-masted and three-
masted vessels, and since it was often difficult to keep a ship with
a square sail on course, a little *mizzen* was soon introduced to
facilitate steering. This was a small three-cornered sail on a mast
aft of the mainmast. This rig we encounter in 1367, on a map by
Pizigano of Venice (194). We can see it in more detail in Gentile
de Fabriano's painting of the early 15th century (195). Notice
that the yard is supported by lifts. The sail has a *bonnet,* a long
strip lashed to the foot of the sail and normally removed when
the wind grew stronger.

In the Maritiem Museum Prins Hendrik in Rotterdam is a model that once hung in a church at Mataró, not far from Barcelona. It was made around the middle of the 15th century, and it
was made as seamen's models often are, even in our own day —
incorrect in its proportions, correct in its details (196—199). It
is the only model we know of from the time when the history of
the great voyages of discovery began — the next known model is
dated a hundred years afterwards.

We see the through-beams, even for the quarter-deck, the curved catena under the forecastle, the *cross and trestle-trees* under
the top, and the triple parrel truck. On either side of the forecastle we see a sheave hole in a clamp, which was later to develop
into the *cathead.* Above all we notice the curved, clinker-fitted
planks under the forecastle, which present such a curious appearance in many pictures (191, 200, 208). The model has only
one mast, but a round hole in the quarter-deck indicates that it
also had a mizzen. The rigging is in complete disorder, but the
parts preserved show that the shrouds were tautened in the southern manner with blocks and lanyards (199).

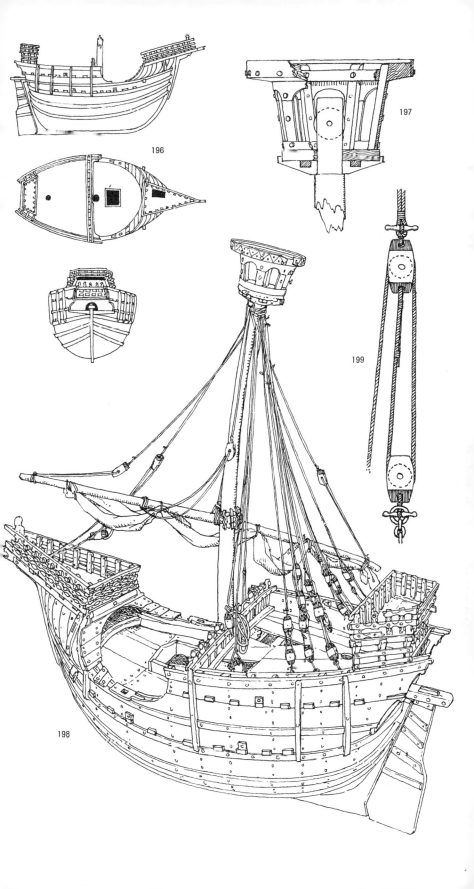

196

197

199

198

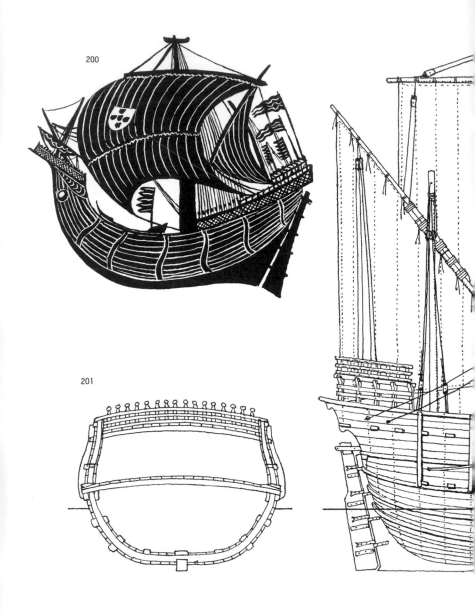

200

201

Probably the earliest representation of a three-masted square-rigged ship is to be found on a Spanish-Moorish bowl made in Malaga in the early 15th century, and showing a Portuguese ship (200) of essentially the same type as the Mataró model (198). The new sail, the *foresail,* on the forecastle, has been lowered, but we can see that it is small, still smaller than the mizzen. These end-sails were still not intended to propel the vessel, they were only

202

steering auxiliaries. The mainmast appears to be very thick, and on larger ships it often consisted of many spars bound together. The shrouds are of southern type, without ratlines. — The reconstruction (201, 202) shows a three-masted vessel from the early 15th century. The details of the hull mainly follow the model from Mataró. A ladder aft of the mast leads to the top.

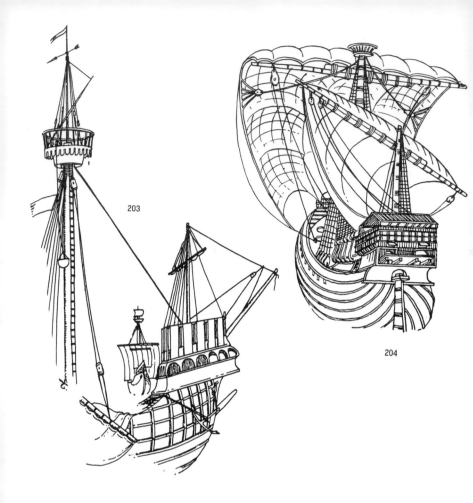

203

204

In a painting by Carpaccio from the end of the 15th century we see a ship (203) carrying a new little sail, the *topsail,* set on the flag-staff of the mainmast and sheeted from the top. A woodcut illustrating Breydenbach's Pilgrimage of 1486 (204) shows a merchantman with a large mizzen, with ratlines in the shrouds and clewlines running from the clews up to blocks on the main yard and down to the deck. It the same picture we find also *martnets,* a strange system of *buntlines* which proceed from the maintop and often continue via a bridle on the front and rear sides of the sail, finally ending in crowfeet around the leeches. When the yard was lowered, the martnets were tightened, drawing the sail together.

More instructive than any of the old pictures is the Flemish master W. A.'s "kraek" from about 1470 (205). "Kraek" is the Flemish way of writing *carrack,* a large, armed round ship. This carrack has two forecastle decks, with supports for an awning above them. A long, new deck is also to be seen above the quarter-

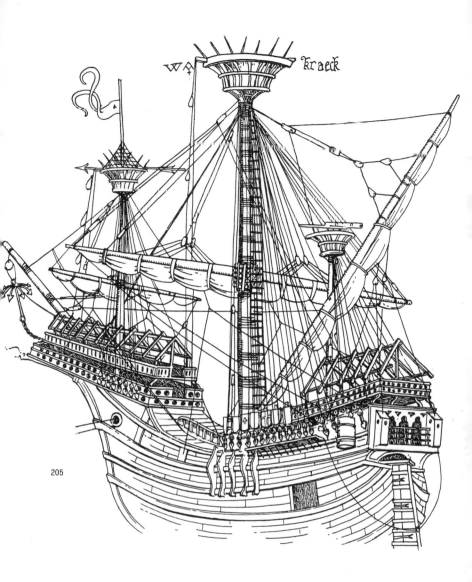

WA   kraeck

205

deck, and aft of the mizzenmast another awning. The main
shrouds are attached in northern fashion to the *channels* with
dead-eyes and lanyards, but they still lack ratlines. The barrel aft
of the channels was for the leadsman. Between the two convenien-
ces in the stern runs an open gallery, and on the quarter-deck
immediately above the barrel we see the muzzles of five guns.
Both the foresail and the mizzen have grown, and are now pro-
pelling sails. The mainyard has double lifts, and the mizzen yard
is supported by a lift to the maintop. Here too we see martnets
from the top down to the mainyard. A bowline from the mainsail runs behind the foremast to a block on the bowsprit. Ammuni-
tion-hoists to the tops, and a swivel-gun on the mizzentop.

206

207

208

The Flemish master W.A. has given us also another picture, which illustrates a further stage of development. On a little N. European merchantman (206), we see behind the foremast a yard with a furled sail, the *spritsail,* which was set when needed under the bowsprit. The majority of pictures from the 15th and 16th century show the spritsail furled, which probably means that it was carried only in special circumstances to improve manoeuvrability. A picture of a Venetian carrack from 1500 (208) shows a fourth mast aft of the mizzenmast, where there was also carried a lateen sail, the *bonaventure mizzen.* Below the bowsprit hangs the spritsail yard. The closely-spaced spars for the awning must have hindered the enemy boarding, and it is probable that a *boarding net*

92

209

was set up over them at this early stage to make it even more difficult. Pictures of Portuguese ships from the early 16th century
(207) show enormous mainsails with double martnets. The topsails, now carried over both main and foretop, have grown, and
are sheeted to the underlying yard.

A painting from the 1520's, probably of the Portuguese giant
carrack *Santa Catarina do Monte Sinai* (209), is very rich in details and shows in different perspectives a further five ships which
seem to be copies of the larger, so that it is possible to make a reconstruction (overleaf) that is more complete in detail than most
of the previous ones. We notice that the topsail sheets are led
down to the deck over the quarter-deck, the *halfdeck*.

93

210

The pictures on these two pages show a century of development
in the rigging of sailing ships. — 210. A little Mediterranean craft
from the early 15th century with mainsail and mizzen. — 211. A
Venetian ship from the end of the same century, with mainsail,
foresail, mizzen and main topsail. — 212. A Venetian carrack
with mainsail, foresail, mizzen, bonaventure, main topsail, and
spritsail. — 213. The Portuguese carrack *Santa Catarina do Monte
Sinai,* in which the numbers indicate: 1. Bonaventure 2. Mizzen

211

212

213

3. Mainsail with two bonnets 4. Foresail with one bonnet 5. Main topsail 6. Fore topsail 7. Spritsail 8. Parrel tackles, which are seen also running from the parrels of the foresail yard 9. Tackles used for lifting boats, guns, spare anchors etc. 10. Topsail sheet 11. Double martnets 12. Tackles for controlling the foot of the mainsail. — The ship has at least six decks and more than 160 guns, the majority of them probably light rail-pieces. She was about 45—50 m. long.

95

214

In the early 16th century, it was common for each maritime nation to build at least one very large ship, as a showpiece, and such was the *Henry Grâce à Dieu,* colloquially known as the *Great Harry.* It was natural, on large ships, to further divide up the sail area, and it was the flaggstaffs over the topmasts that carried the new *toppgallants.* The sources relate that the English ship *Regent* carried topgallants on the mainmast and topsails on the three other masts as early as 1509. When the *Henry Grâce à Dieu* was built in 1514, she was rigged with topmasts and topgallant masts on the forward three and a topmast on the bonaventure. She was fitted with 184 guns, presumably quite light. Unfortunately there is no contemporary picture of her.

She was almost wholly rebuilt during the years 1536–39 and in 1545 was depicted in her new shape by an Officer of the Ordnance, Anthony Anthony (214). We see that she was square-sterned, unlike previous large ships, and it is possible that sterns were first shaped in this way in the 16th century. I know of no 15th century material showing an unambiguously square-sterned vessel. The picture portrays her with a topgallant even on the bonaventure, but we do not know whether this is to be believed. The main and foremast yards have sharp hooks on the arms, to tear apart the rigging of enemy ships at close quarters. A boarding-grapnel hangs from the crowned end of the long bowsprit. After

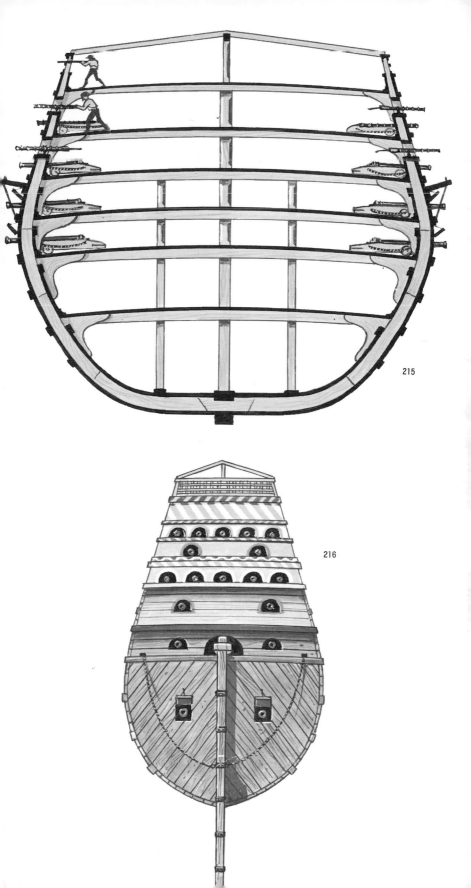

215

216

217

rebuilding she was fitted with 21 heavy bronze guns, 130 iron guns and 100 hand-guns. We see that she carried her heavy guns on two complete decks.

It is difficult to reconstruct the *Henry Grâce à Dieu*. Guided by the painting I have assumed that she had six decks aft of the mainmast (215—217). The lowest was the orlop deck. Then came the gun deck and main deck, where the heaviest guns were posi-

tioned. Lighter guns and rail-pieces were set up on the quarter-deck and the next. Soldiers with light weapons stood on the upper deck which was covered with a boarding net.

On a painting depicting the departure of Henry VIII from Dover in 1520, *Henry Grâce à Dieu* is to be seen with yellow sails painted so as to simulate cloth of gold. In the reconstruction I have given her similar sails.

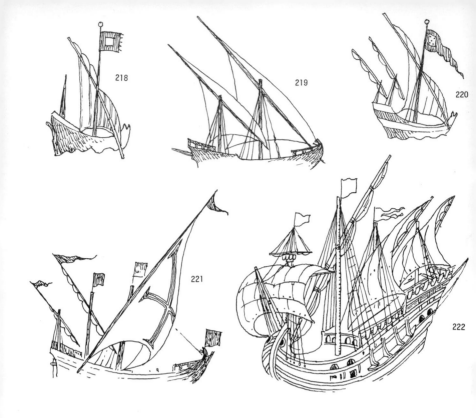

The caravel

The caravel is associated mainly with the days of the great voyages of discovery, and we know that such vessels were used for exploration along the west coast of Africa in the early 15th century. We know almost nothing of their origin, and very little of their details. The word *caravela* occurs in a Portuguese manuscript dated 1255 as a name for fishing boats. Some of the hulls in extant pictures of caravels, all from the 16th century (218—222), also resemble !arge boats rather than ships.

The early caravels carried lateen sails on two or three masts, but towards the end of the 15th century they were often fitted, in Spain at least, with the usual ship's rigging, with a square foresail and mainsail and a lateen mizzen. Possibly the caravel was square-sterned from the very beginning, but we have no clear evidence of this. It had a more shallow draught than the usual round ship, and was relatively faster. Reconstructions of caravels from the early 16th century (223—224) are based on an excessive amount of guesswork. The reconstruction of a caravel of 1545 (225), based on a drawing of the same year (222), is somewhat more authoritative.

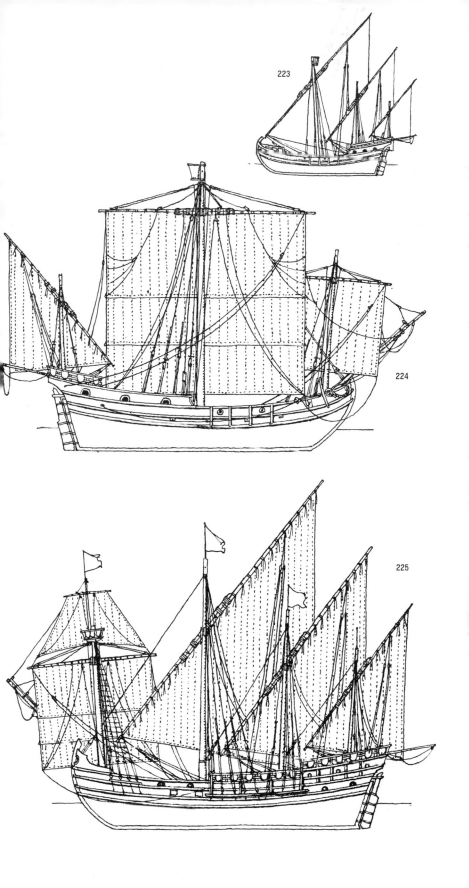

223

224

225

226

The galleon

Of perhaps even more obscure origin than the caravel is the *galleon*. We usually connect it with Spain, and it is possible that it did come from that country, but in that case it must have spread very quickly because we find it in England, France and Italy alike by the mid 16th century. The type of ship represented by the early galleons seems to have made its appearance as a protest against the broad and ever more towering carracks.

The word *galleon* is perhaps related to *galley,* and a Venetian manuscript from 1550 describes "a galleon propelled by oars", but we can guess that the vessel in question was a *galeass*. The

early, admittedly unclear pictures existing of Portuguese galleons from 1535, and above all the copy of a 1540 model which is in the Museo Naval at Madrid (226), represent pure sailing-ships with no trace of oars. The Venetian manuscript also gives the dimensions of a large *sailing* galleon; length from stem to stern 135 1/2 feet, length of keel 100 feet, beam 33 feet, giving the rough proportions 4:3:1. As a rule the carracks had 3:2:1.

But slimness was not the only characteristic of the new type. On the carracks the high forecastle projected far out over the bow (cf. 213, 217). On the galleons the castle was within the bows, and proceeding from the hull itself — as a sort of continuation of the deck and bulwarks — there was a projecting part later to be called the *beak-head*. In its early stages this projection resembled the ram of the galleys, and it is possibly this that gave rise to the name of galleon.

The reconstruction (227) shows a Spanish galleon from the same period as the model. Midships over the boarding net is a *gangway* from the quarter-deck directly to the forecastle deck. The projection over the bow, the beak-head, facilitates handling the spritsail. The insignia of Emperor Charles V are painted on the mainsail. Like all larger ships of those times, the galleon carries four masts.

103

Drawings from engravings by Pieter Breughel the Elder, 1565.
— 228 Warship (galleon ?) with ram. — 229. Galleon running
under its foresail alone. Towards the end of the century, complicated details of rigging began to appear, with many crowfeet
ends at spars, stays and leeches. Their real purpose was to even

the pull, but on naval ships in particular they were to become merely decorative ends in themselves. The long clumsy after-castle has been inherited from the carracks. Some of Breughel's rigging details are incomplete.

A manuscript from the late 16th century includes some constructional drawings of Elizabethan warships (230—232), probably made in 1586 by the master shipwright Matthew Baker. They show very clearly the dimensions, shape and appearance of these vessels. The most outstanding ships in the English fleet which in 1588 beat the Great Armada must have resembled the ships in this manuscript (reconstruction 233).

Baker's galleons are low and elegant for the time. The long beak-head is supported by a knee, divided above, on the leading edge of the stem-post, a *cutwater*. The *figurehead* appears to be a dragon. The forecastle is composed of a single deck, but the galleon has both quarter-deck, half deck and *poop deck*. On the diagram of sails (230), both mizzens extend a little beyond the yard-arms, causing us to believe that they were fitted with bonnets.

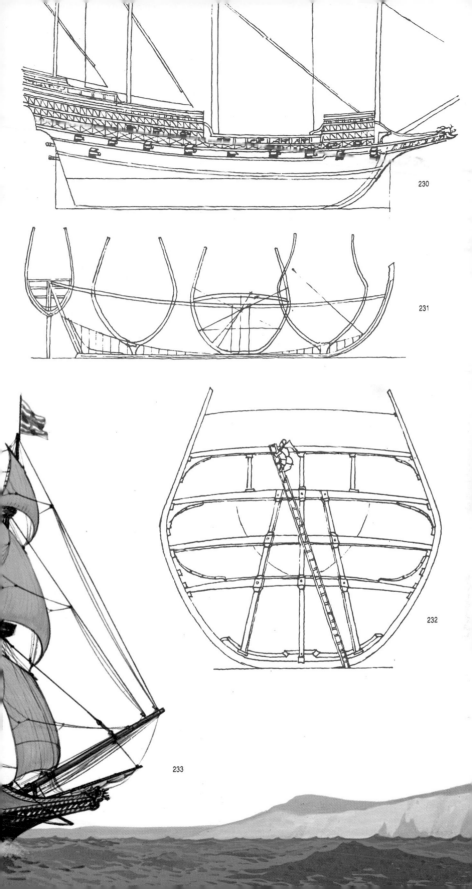

230

231

232

233

234. Dutch East Indiaman according to a picture of 1597. — 235.
Small galleon of the same type, according to an engraving of the
same period. This has a single forecastle deck, quarter-deck and
half deck. A gallery over the stern, and a bit forward on either
quarter. The arched opening in front of the mizzenmast is the
helmsman's "window". — 236. *Whipstaff* in use. Previously the
helmsman or helmsmen of larger vessels had stood under the half
deck, steering by compass and command and managing the long

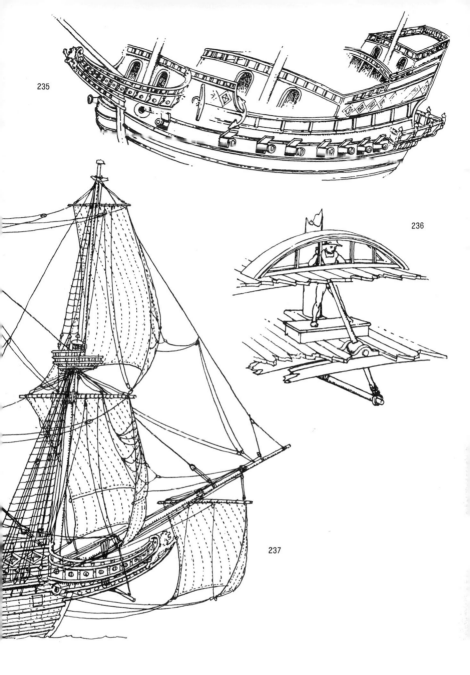

235

236

237

tiller with tackles. With the help of the whipstaff, the helmsman on larger ships could now observe the sails when steering, which was important particularly when going to windward. The angle of the rudder was not large, and for major changes of course the ship was trimmed by the sails. — 237. Reconstruction of a Dutch galleon from the end of the 16th century. Notice the sensible, sparing use of crowfeet in the rigging.

The most beautiful model we have of a 16th century ship is to be found in the Museo Naval in Madrid, a Flemish galleon from 1593 (238). It has been damaged and the rigging inexpertly repaired. With proportions according to Matthew Baker I have made a reconstruction (239) with exactly the same ornamentation as on the model.

Only the lower masts are raised. As on most 16th century vessels, the foremast is situated forward of the forecastle. Close up under the mast and at a level with the main deck we see the *cathead*. A boarding net is set up over the main deck, and at the level of of the bulwark a gangway with rail runs on each side. The long carved gallery begins at the aftermost channel and curves right round the stern. The entire space between the gun decks is carved and gilded. The remaining ornamentation is painted.

Within less than two hundred years, the sailing-ship had undergone a more profound development than during the preceding

110

239

5,000 years, and more than was to occur in the remaining 350 years to come. The one-masted ship had swiftly become two and three-masted, had been given spritsail and topsails, was fitted with a fourth mast, and later also with topgallants. The monstrously high carracks were motivated as long as sea battles consisted almost exclusively of boarding. When more effective guns permitted fire from a distance, the carrack was swiftly replaced by the galleon, the predecessor of the ship of the line.

The art of shipbuilding was still no science. Ships were built with regard simply to certain basic dimensions and norms when forming the keel and frames. Attempts were made to copy the vessels that had proved to be good sailers, and there was a certain understanding of the importance of the shape and dimensions of the hull for seaworthiness. Some shipbuilders who were gifted in such matters recorded their rules and norms and, like Matthew Baker, illustrated their manuscripts with explanatory drawings.

241

240

Galleys and galeasses

We know that the warships of classical times were rowed by oars in two or three banks, and with one or more oarsmen to each oar. In the early Middle Ages, perhaps even in the 14th century, the Byzantine dromons at least were still rowed by two banks of oars.

A painting from Siena of the late 14th century shows fighting galleys (detail 240). These primitively portrayed warships show that the oars were in groups of two, but in one plane over an out-rigger, or *apostis*. In principle these galleys differ very little from the late Greek bireme (cf. 92, 107). A broken stern-rudder seems to be lying below the platform in the stern.

We know that the trading cities of Italy had their merchant galleys, and such a vessel is depicted in a manuscript from the middle of the 15th century (244), a three-masted ship with nine-teen groups of three oars on either side, making altogether 114 oars and oarsmen. In the 15th and 16th centuries, naval galleys usually carried only one mast with a lateen sail, as shown in the picture from 1482 (242). In about 1490, Carpaccio painted a large galley (241), in which we can count 84 rowlocks, in groups of three, which means 84 oars on either side and a total of 168. The

242

reconstruction (243) shows the forepart of a 15th century galley, with one man to each oar. The thwarts lay obliquely, as I believe they were on the later Greek rowing vessels. Between the oarsmen runs a long bridge, the *corsia,* from stem to stern, really a raised part of the hull whose sturdy side planks give much strength to the vessel fore-and-aft.

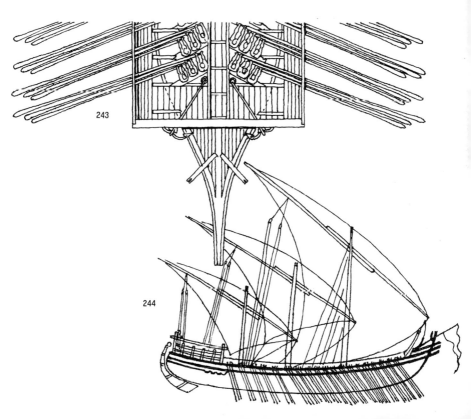

243

244

At the beginning of the 16th century — perhaps earlier — a new and better system of propulsion was introduced. Rowing was found to be simpler and more efficient if the number of oars was reduced and several men, usually five, placed on each oar. A painting of about 1510 in Siena shows a large *galeass* (245), a cross between a galley and a large sailing vessel, where the oars now rest evenly spaced on the apostis, indicating that the new system had come into use. Pieter Breughel the Elder shows us in 1565 a galley (246) with seven guns on the foredeck. A large gun lay amidships on the corsia, and was aimed laterally by turning

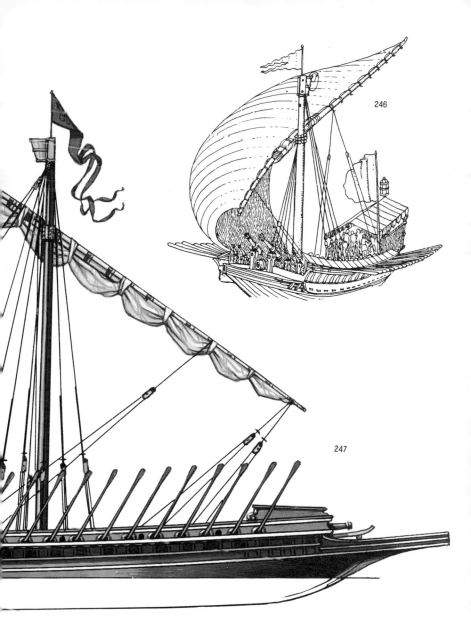

246

247

the whole galley. The other guns are light swivel-guns on heavy posts.

A greatly damaged model and paintings in the Doge's Palace in Venice have furnished the basis of a reconstruction of a Venetian galley from the mid 16th century (247). The tent, the lantern, and long flagstaff on the after-castle were to survive until the last days of the galleys. Above the guns on the foredeck is a short fighting deck. The galley was presumably rowed by 240 men at 48 oars.

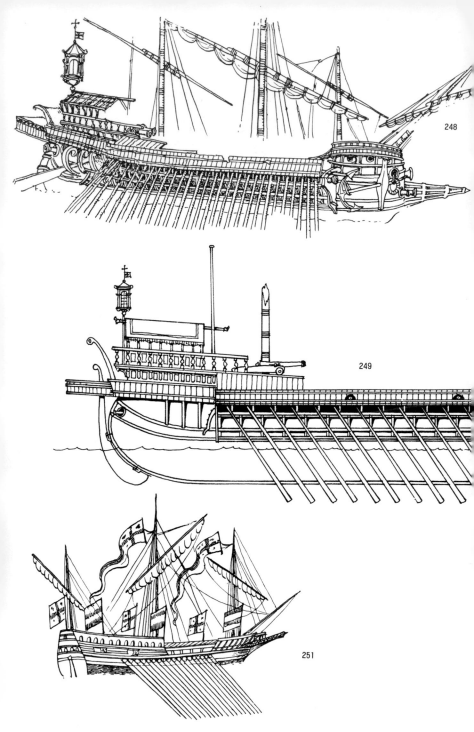

Contemporary portrayals of the great galley-fight at Lepanto in
1571 concentrate on the heavy, powerful galeasses (248). In these
an attempt had been made at combining the manoeuvrability
and independence of wind of the galley with a heavy ship's
strength, capacity for carrying guns, and ability to sail when

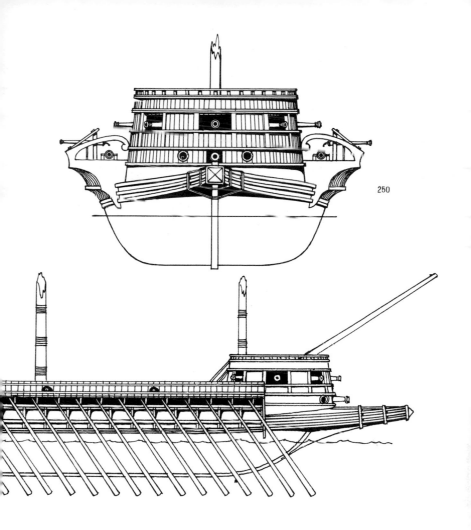

250

necessary. A Venetian manuscript from the mid 16th century gives us the dimensions of "rowing galleons", perhaps galeasses. The largest of these was 145 feet from stem to stern-post, 27 feet wide and 9 feet deep. The reconstruction (249, 250) has been based on the galeass at Lepanto, and the Venetian measurements. We can count eight heavy guns in the forecastle, and two more heavy pieces on carriages in the after-castle, plus 12—14 lighter guns. As on Breughel's galley (246), the oarsmen are protected by a long, sloping breastwork. The ram appears to be powerful and shod in iron, so that it could still be used for its old purpose.

In Anthony Anthony's illustrations of the vessels in the English fleet of 1545 there are also galeasses (251), but, exactly as one might have expected of a northern country, unfamiliar with galleys, what was built was a sailing-ship, perhaps a little longer and lower than usual, which had been fitted with oars.

During the 17th century, the Mediterranean galeass underwent no major change. A galeass from 1699 (252) was propelled by 300 or 350 oarsmen at 50 oars. It carried lateen sails on three masts, and a bowsprit with spritsail. The ram has gone, and its place has been taken by a beak-head typical of the sailing-ships of those days.

In comparison with the broadsides that could be fired by the large sailing-ships, the armament of the galeass seems to be remarkably weak. It carried rarely more than twenty guns. Pictures of galeasses from the same period appear to show up to fifty guns, but they are mostly small swivel-guns. Both the galley and

252

the galeass had really become outmoded during the 16th century, and that they continued to be built probably depended mainly on the dogmatic belief that sea-fights in the Mediterranean, with its few winds, could only be carried out with oar-propelled vessels.

During the 17th century, France became the leading power in Europe, and Louis XIV built a modern navy to compete with the English and Dutch. The majority of his ships were pure sailing-ships, intended for use along the Atlantic coast of France. Galleys and galeasses, however, were also built to secure the nation's interests off the long Mediterranean coast.

119

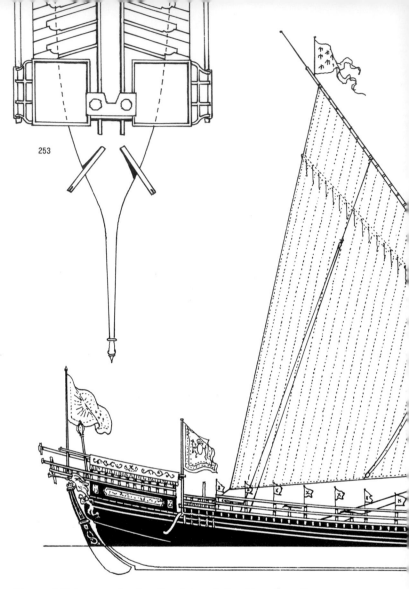

253

From 1526 onwards the flagship of the French galley commander was called *La Réale*, which meant that she was the property of
the king, and carried the flags of both the king and her commander. The 17th century French galleys were classified as *ordinary*
with 26 pairs of thwarts and *extraordinary* which could have as
many as 33 pairs. Normally a galley had 5 oarsmen on each
thwart, but the very largest, including of course the *réales*, could
have up to 7 men per thwart, thus being driven by a total of 462
galley-slaves.

A *réale* from the end of the 17th century (253—256) measured
about 52 m. at the waterline, was 6.4 m. wide, and had 31 pairs
of thwarts minus one, one of them on the port side being taken
up by the cook's galley. The oarsmen numbered 427. The two

254

lateen sails combined were of 750 sq.m. The hull had very low sides, and waves washed up on deck in the slighest sea. When sailing in a good wind, the leeside of the deck lay under water, and the oarsmen often sat in the wet up to their waists.

The sails were always furled before battle, and the yards were made safe to the masts with chains so that they could not so easily be shot down and interfere with manoeuvring the vessel. If the wind was fresh, a galley would avoid giving battle to a sailing-ship. Because of their length they were very slow on the turn, and experiments were made in the 18th century with an additional rudder in the bows. Only in calm weather did the galleys have a chance against pure sailing-ships, when they could turn from the broadsides and choose the position of battle themselves.

121

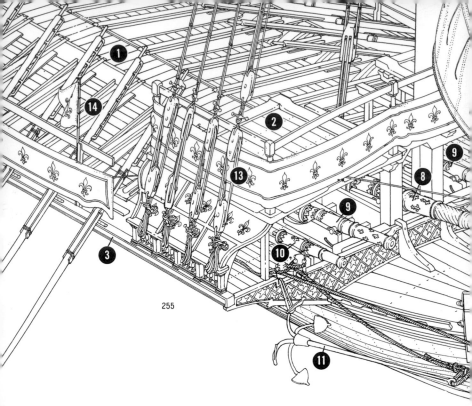

255

Shown here is the forepart of the *réale* in perspective (255), and a section of the ship immediately forward of the mainmast (256). The heaviest guns were situated under the forecastle (2), and consisted of five bronze pieces. The largest gun (8) was a 36-pounder which was called a *coursier* as it was mounted on the corsia (French *coursie*). It could be aimed horizontally only by turning the entire galley. On either side of the coursier stood two 24-pounder *batards* (9) and two 18-pounder *moyennes* (10). The measurement in pounds denoted the size of the gun and the weight of the ball it fired. A 36-pounder fired a ball weighing 36 pounds, and so on. Twelve swivel guns were mounted on the catwalks running outside the oarsmen (7).

The coursie (1) ran between the thwarts over the very rounded deck where the driver's two assistants walked with their whips and encouraged the oarsmen, who were either criminals sentenced to the galleys or prisoners of war. To make it easier to identify them in the event of attempted escape, their heads were shaven to leave only a small tuft on top. Below the narrow thwarts (4) was a stretcher (5) for the feet and a broader thwart (6) where the slaves sat while at rest and when the vessel was under sail. The long oars which rested on the apostis (3) had seven handles (14).

122 The narrow gangway inside the apostis (7) was where the crew and soldiers were positioned. The forecastle (2) consisted of a

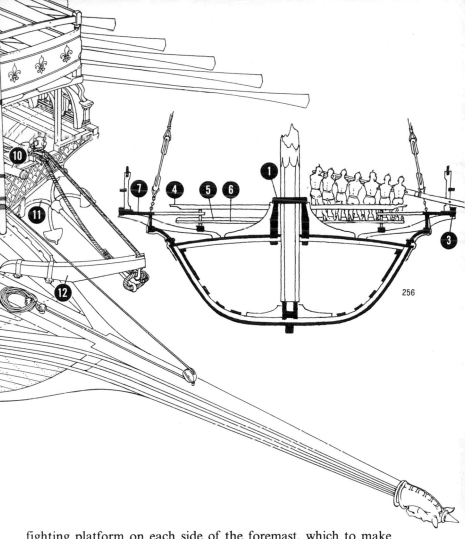

256

fighting platform on each side of the foremast, which to make room for the coursier stood at the side of the coursie, while the mainmast stood in the middle of the coursie. The large open after-castle or poop, as it was called on galleys, was traditionally covered with a splendid awning, supported by horizontal spars. As in all Mediterranean lateeners, the shrouds were tightened with lanyards (13). The curved catheads (12) existed on galleys from as early as the 15th century (cf. 241), as did the long grapnel-shaped anchors (11).

Proceeding from the stern the layout of the galley under deck began with the captain's cabin, then a smaller room for the belongings of the officers, a store for drink and fresh food, and then another store for dry foodstuffs. Amidships was a locker for reserve sails and a large awning which could be rigged up over the whole galley when in port. Forward of the mast was the powder magazine, and farthest forward the cable locker.

123

Sailing ships from N. Europe, 17th century

Nothing really sensational occurred in the development of the ship during the 17th century, but this is when reliable sources begin to appear in the form of paintings, engravings and drawings which reproduce vessels in exact proportion. We have detailed models to scale, and we have also the Swedish royal ship *Vasa* of 1628, which was raised from the harbour of Stockholm in 1961 and is still being restored at the time of writing.

A Dutch engraving from 1613 which is supposed to be the first showing a ship with three complete gun decks, the English *Prince Royal,* seems to be a purely imaginative vessel drawn up on Dutch originals. With this as a model I have drawn a ship (257) which might be representative of a large Dutch man-of-war. It has double galleries and small turrets round the after-castle, and right out at the end of the bowsprit is an innovation: a mast has developed out of the flagstaff (cf. 217), to carry a new sail, the *spritsail topsail.*

A Dutch East Indiaman from the same period (258) shows a simplified rigging, in which the inconvenient lateen topsail on the mizzenmast has disappeared. The English ship *Red Lion* (259) is to be found on a large painting by Hendrik Vroom, together with the famous *Prince Royal* (260). The *Red Lion* was an old

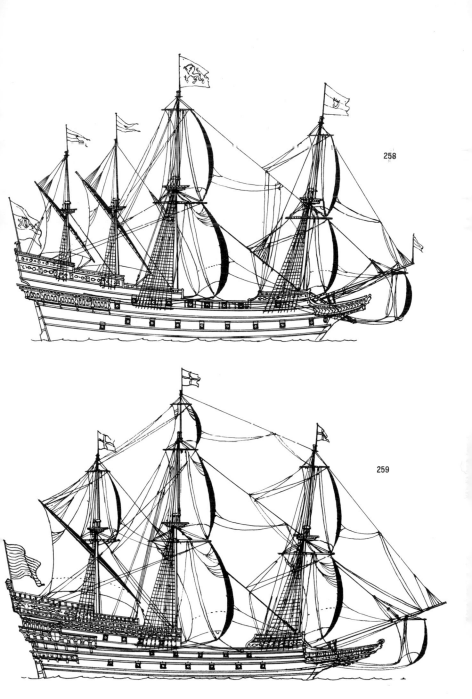

258

259

ship which was rebuilt in 1609 and then fitted with a *mizzen top-sail* which was no longer a lateen but a square sail between two yards, the *mizzen topsail yard* and the *crojack yard*. The picture shows also a furled sail on the crojack yard, but no future illustrations have such sails and we can assume that Vroom painted a sail there by mistake.

125

The *Prince Royal* was built in 1610 by the renowned Phineas Pett, a man of an old shipbuilding family, of excellent technical education for his time, and one of the foremost master shipbuilders known to history. The above picture is based on a painting by Hendrik Vroom from 1620. She had three complete gun decks with a total of 56 guns. Later she was rebuilt twice, finally to be armed with 90 guns. She had three galleries, but the two uppermost were connected with a row of windows and the large coat-of-

arms with the three plumes of the Prince of Wales. She carried the new type of mizzen topsail on both the mizzenmast proper and the bonaventure mast. She was about 210 feet long, 43 1/2 feet wide, and was the largest ship of her time. The greater part of her carving was gilt on a green background. Her carvings cost £441 0s 4d, while the painting and gilding went to as much as £868 6s 8d.

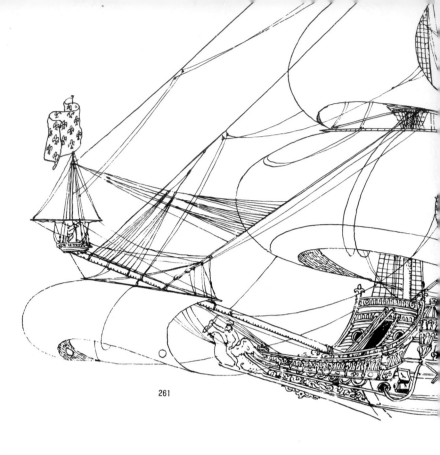

261

Hendrik Hondius' engraving from 1626, here redrawn for the sake of clarity (261), probably depicts the French *Saint Louis,* which was built in Holland. Since boarding was no longer common and sea battles involved mainly exchanges of gunnery, the boarding net could be dispensed with. The gangway between the quarter deck and forecastle grew instead into a broad grating deck, supported by arched beams.

When the Swedish Royal ship *Vasa* was lifted from the Port of Stockholm in 1961, it was a severely damaged hull that saw the light of day. The entire figurehead was torn away, as was the af-

262

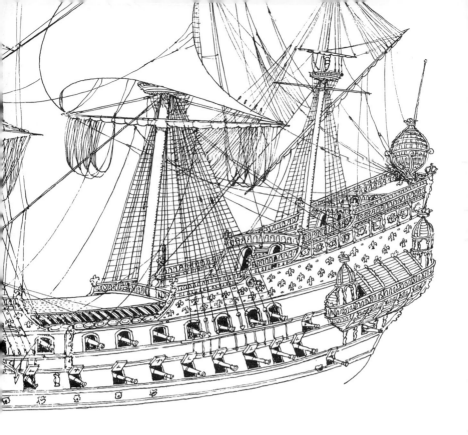

ter-castle with its carved stern and any galleries. Even before the ship was lifted, numerous carved details had been found lying loose, including carved lions from the hatches to the gun ports (262); the *Vasa* was thus known to have been unusually ornate. Subsequent diving until 1968 revealed thousands of details that in the course of three centuries had been torn loose and sunk into the mud. After intensive research and jig-saw puzzle work, it is now known approximately where each part sat, so that it will be possible to rebuild the ship practically in its entirety.

Hendrik Hondius' engraving has been a great help to those fitting together the pieces of the *Vasa,* just as it was probably a pattern for those who originally built and decorated the ship. But a model exists in order to be surpassed. The carved details of the *Vasa* provided a gallery almost exactly like that on the *Saint Louis,* but there were pieces over for another gallery above the first (see overleaf). Nor were the builders content with a gangway; they combined the quarter-deck and forecastle with a real deck so as to form a long upper deck (see pp. 132—133).

263

This is how the *Vasa* looked in 1628. The blue colour on parts
of the ship is sheer guesswork. The rigging is drawn mostly from
Hondius' engraving and other contemporary pictures. The main
mast, however, is entirely preserved, as are many sails, so that
we know the proportions of the rigging. The strong slant of the

main mast is surprising, as is the forward inclination of the tops. The position of the top, however, is clearly shown by tracks in the mast. The length of the figurehead fits the picture of the *Saint Louis* although Hondius was previously thought to have exaggerated. The lantern has not been recovered, and is drawn

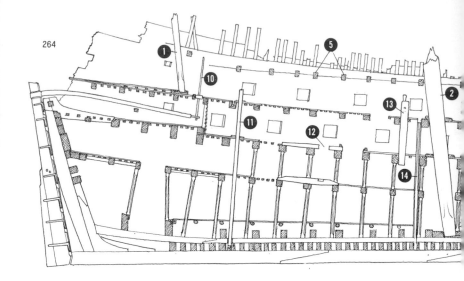

from the *Saint Louis*. The flags and pennants are drawn from somewhat later pictures.

The *Vasa* was built by a Dutchman, Hendrik Hybertsson, and measurements show her to have been designed along well established Dutch lines. That she was still so unstable as to heel over and sink on her maiden voyage may have been due to the great weight of her hull, the excessive weight above her water line. We have no contemporary vessels with which to compare her, but a drawing from twenty years later suggests that the *Vasa* was unusually powerfully built. From stem to stern and up along her entire side the ribs are close together, with practically no room in between, and her beams and knees are very large. It was probably intended originally to have lighter guns on her upper gun deck, as the ports there are smaller than on the lower; in the end, however, the *Vasa* was armed with 24-pounders on both decks, which must further have impaired her stability.

The drawings show the *Vasa* in section from stem to stern at the time she was salvaged (264), and in cross section with a reconstruction of the upper deck (265). 1. Mizzen mast 2. Main mast 3. Foremast 4. Bowsprit 5. Beams for upper deck. The missing beams have subsequently been recovered, as has most of the decking. The middle of the deck is covered with gratings for ventilation 6. Upper gundeck with gratings for ventilation 7. Lower gundeck 8. Main deck 9. Provision floor. Below this was stowed the stone ballast 10. Whipstaff (cf. p. 109) 11. Pump 12. Space for large capstan 13. Knight for hoisting the mainyard 14. Pump 15. Capstan 16. Riding bitt 17. Brick galley. There was no stack, and the smoke escaped freely.

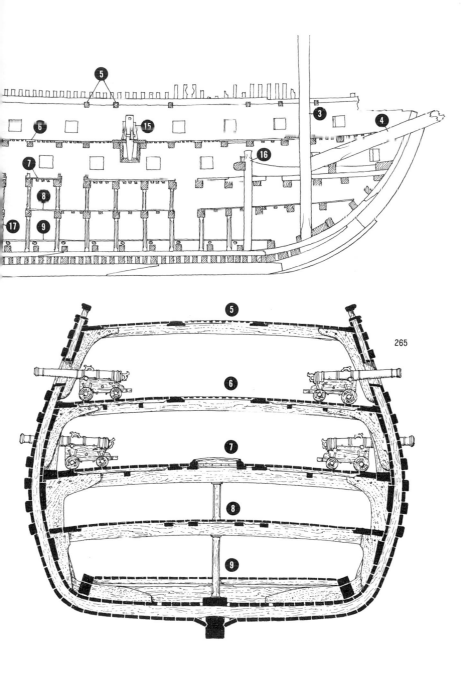

265

The total length of the *Vasa* is 60.5 m. Length between perpendiculars 47.5 m., length of keel 38.5 m., greatest breadth 11 m. Draught abt. 4.7 m., displacement 1,300 tons, sail area 1,200 sq.m. Armament: forty-eight 24-pounders, eight 3 pounders, two 1-pounders, and six light boarding pieces. Crew: 3 officers, 12 commissioned officers, 12 artisans, 90 seamen, 20 gunners, 300 soldiers.

On 26th July 1634 Charles I visited his shipyards at Woolwich and ordered Phineas Pett to build the largest ship ever seen. She was to measure 124 feet in the keel, 46 feet in the beam, and have a draught of 22 feet. A couple of weeks later, Trinity House, representative of all nautical expertise, protested against the decision of the king and stated that such a vessel would be unmanageable and could not be used in English waters.

The king, however, was determined to have his giant at any price, and in fact she came to be even larger than imagined: 127 feet in the keel, 48 feet wide, and a draught of 23 1/2 feet. At the time a ship of 40 guns cost about £6,000. When she was ready, the *Sovereign of the Seas,* as the new giant was named, cost a total of £65,586 16s 9 1/2d.

She was launched in 1637. It is often asserted that she was the first ship to carry *royals,* a sail above the topgallant; however, a manuscript from 1625 states that flagpoles could also carry royals, and a painting in Udbyneder Church in Denmark, from 1525, shows such a sail on the mainmast. This, on the other hand, may just have been the painter's imagination. In size, at any rate, the *Sovereign* was a hundred and fifty years before her time. She carried 100 guns and could very well have been included in Nel-

son's fleet as a first rate ship of the line. And if she was superior to all previous ships as to size and armament, she was also superior in another way to all ships that were to come after her: she was the most richly decorated ship in the world.

Her ornamentation was carved from sketches by van Dyck. All her decorations and carvings were in gold leaf, and the Dutch who kept their distance from her in many sea battles called her "The Golden Devil".

From the beginning of the 16th century a square stern had been common on all the larger European men-of-war, but the stern of the *Sovereign* was made round, first flattening out ten feet above the waterline. Such sterns were to be characteristic of English men-of-war well into the 19th century, while the Dutch and French retained the square stern (cf. 271).

The *Sovereign of the Seas* was later rebuilt many times, and a large proportion of her upperwork and decoration was cut down, since she lay so deep that it was nearly impossible to use the lowest leeside battery when only heeling over slightly. She was finally rechristened to the *Royal Sovereign*. She took a very honourable part in many sea-fights and was never defeated, but an over-turned candle sealed her fate in 1696 and she went up in flames.

135

The *Sovereign of the Seas'* rig as it appears in J. Payne's well-known engraving is shown here in reconstruction. The length of the top yard is about half of the course yard, the length of the topgallant yard a half of the top yard, and that of the royal yard half of the topgallant yard.

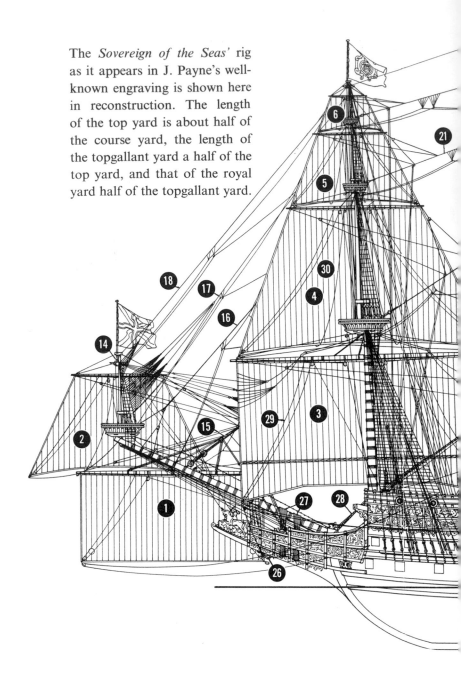

1. Spritsail 2. Spritsail topsail 3. Foresail with bonnet 4. Fore topsail 5. Fore topgallant 6. Fore royal 7. Mainsail, furled. The martnets hang below the yard 8. Main topsail 9. Main topgallant 10. Main royal 11. Mizzen topsail 12. Mizzen topgallant 13. Mizzen with bonnet 14. Spritsail topmast 15. Forestay 16. Fore topmast stay 17. Fore topgallant stay 18. Fore royal stay 19. Mainstay

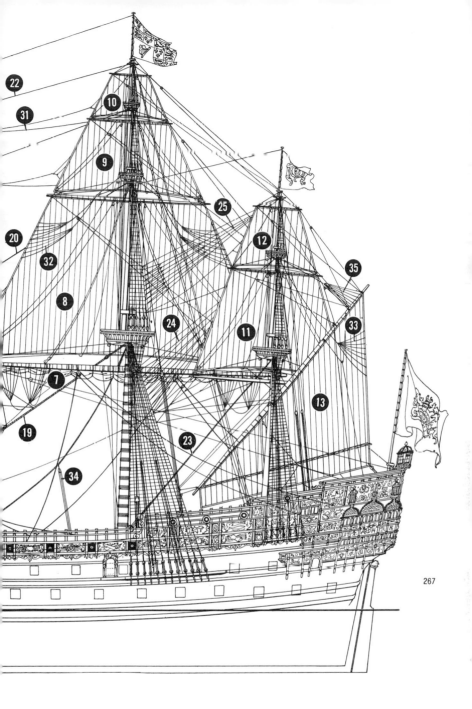

20. Main topmast stay 21. Main topgallant stay 22. Main royal stay 23. Mizzen stay 24. Mizzen topmast stay 25. Mizzen topgallant stay 26. Fairleads for the fore tacks 27. Gammonings 28. Mainstay collar 29. Clewgarnet 30. Buntline 31. Bowlines 32. Martnets 33. Mizzen martnet 34. Winding tackle 35. Mizzen lift.   137

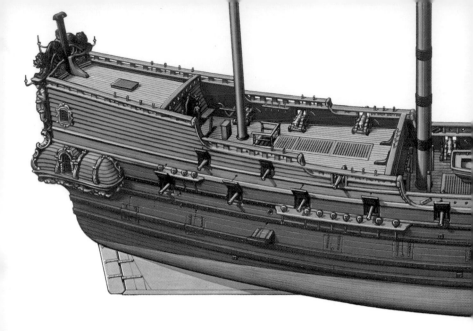

While England and France built many three-decked ships during the 17th century, the Dutch built only a few. The most common Dutch man-of-war had two gun decks, presumably because the Dutch preferred shallow-draught vessels. Their ships were also lighter built in proportion to the English, and even if they were faster and more easily manoeuvred the light construction often proved disastrous in exchanges of gunfire. Even so, Dutch ship-building came to be the model for many foreign powers. Peter the Great made a personal study of shipbuilding at Zaandam in Holland in 1697, and Frenchmen, Swedes, Danes and Germans had earlier profited from Dutch skill.

Outwardly the Dutch ships differed from the English and French in their comparatively sparse ornamentation. During the 17th century the beak-head gradually curved upwards more and more, mainly because a low beak-head, especially on smaller vessels, became too "wet". The beak-head had long functioned as the heads for the crew.

The quarter galleries in the stern which had become the officers' toilets were completely covered in with clinker-laid planks. The planking of the poop and the upper part of the bulwarks around the half deck were also clinker-laid, to combine lightness with strength. The stern was decorated with a coat-of-arms framed in the various ornamentations of Dutch baroque architecture with lions, soldiers, cupids and caryatids bearing friezes, convolutes and other whorls.

268

On many ships the whipstaff (cf. 236) was brought up through the quarter-deck so that the helmsman could be outside. In the picture (268) the whipstaff can be seen immediately forward of the entrance to the poop, and between it and the mizzenmast is the compass in its *binnacle*. The rails are raised amidships into a breastwork with apertures for the barrels of the soldiers' hand-guns. On the forecastle, amidships and on the half deck there are large V-shaped *cavils* for securing the sheets.

269

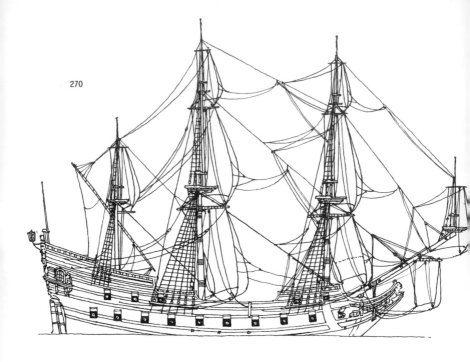

We hear of "frigates", small swift craft armed with 6—12 guns, as early as the beginning of the 17th century, but soon both the vessels and their armament were to grow so that by the middle of the century we hear of an English frigate of 64 guns. During the 17th century, however, a frigate usually meant a full-rigged man-of-war with only one complete gun deck. The picture (270) shows a Dutch frigate of 1665.

For some unknown reason reef-points do not seem to have been used on larger vessels for a period of more than a hundred years. We have seen them on Nordic seals into the 15th century, and they occur into the beginning of the following century, but then they vanish. They make their return about 1660 on the large topsails (271). Note how the yard has been lengthened, to be able to reef the very tapering sails. A reefline runs to the yardarm from a cringle in the sail. — The lifts of the main and top yards run through *fiddle blocks* (blocks with two sheaves after one another) and the sheets of the topgallant and topsail are rove through the same blocks and from there through a block on the yard near the mast down to the deck.

Under the top yard hangs a *foot rope* for support while furling the sail. This appears to have come into use about the same time as the reef-points in the topsail, around 1660. The picture is of the Dutch ship *Gouda,* built in 1665. At the beginning of the century, ships usually carried one lantern over the stern. Later three became common, and occasionally five were carried.

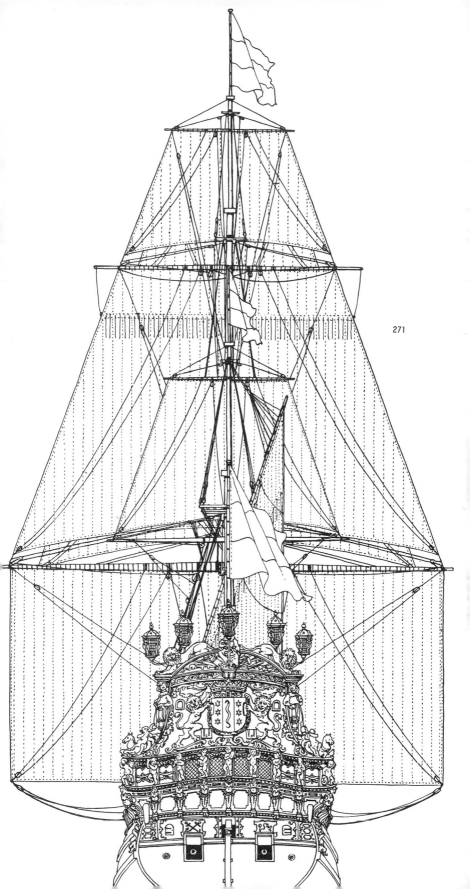

271

In England about 1660 it became common to build models of the larger ships planned and to send them to the king and admiralty for approval before the actual vessels were built. One of the oldest admiralty models extant is of the 100-gun ship *Prince* of 1670 (272). We see that the cat-heads, the wreaths around the gunports, and nearly all ornamentation are gilt on a black background. But what is gilt on the models was usually yellow paint

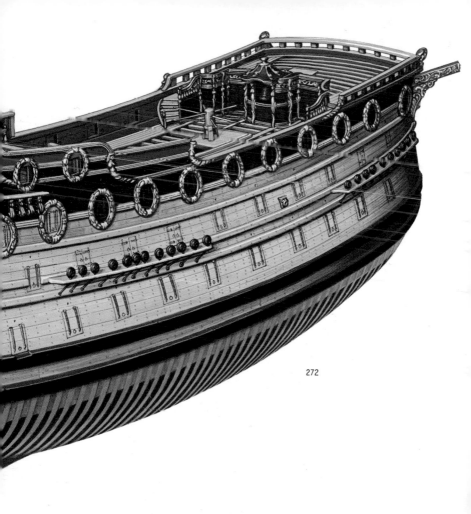

272

in reality, and only the royal arms always to be found on the sterns of the English ships was accorded true gilding.

Right up until the middle of the 17th century all the ships of varying size and ornament which constituted a fleet had fought without any real order of battle. In 1653, however, the British Admiralty issued an order that ships were to give battle in line, in single file that is to say, so that broadsides would be most effective. This presupposed that the ships would be able to sail at about the same speed and that they were approximately equally armed, otherwise a more weakly armed vessel in the line might be forced to fight with a superior enemy.

Ships were therefore divided into rates. A first rate ship had over 90 guns, a second over 80 and a third rate over 50. These first three rates were considered strong enough to fight in the line and were therefore called *ships of the line*. A fourth rate ship had over 38 guns, a fifth over 18, and finally a sixth over 6.

143

273

It is recorded that Holland at the beginning of the 17th century had over 10,000 merchantmen of different kinds, and we know that 55 per cent of all ships that passed Øresund and were controlled by the Danish Customs at Elsinore were Dutchmen. The

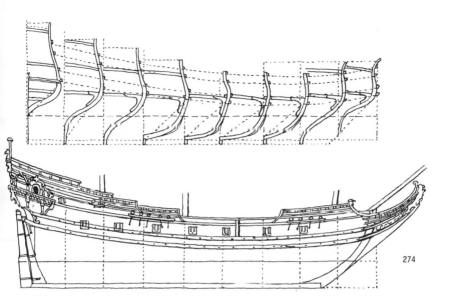

274

most important merchantman, in European waters anyway, seems
to have been the *fluyt* (273), a round-sterned, flat-bottomed and
relatively narrow vessel. As the Øresund duty was based on ton-
nage which was calculated among other things by the bulk of the
vessel amidships, the 17th century fluyts were built with the sides
sloping sharply inwards. A new system of measurement, however, was introduced in 1669, and from then on the decks of the
fluyts gradually became broader.

Around the middle of the century the topsails of all vessels had
become so much larger that they were soon to outgrow the course.
Many ships, both merchantmen and warships, sailed without topgallants, and because of the great demand for seamen the Dutch
ships were made so easy to handle that as early as 1603 Sir Walter
Raleigh complained that where an English ship of 100 tons needed
a crew of 30 a corresponding Dutch ship could make do with 10.

The *pinnace* was used both for warfare and for trading. As op-
posed to the fluyt it was flat-sterned, and it differed from an ordinary full-rigged ship only in being smaller. Perhaps the oldest
constructional drawing in the modern sense with the ribs included so that we can form a clear idea of the shape of the hull
is of a pinnace of 1670 (274). It has one single deck, a short quarter-deck, half deck and a high forecastle, but the bulwarks, which
are high around the open deck, hide all sharp contours and
create a very harmonious little vessel. There were also larger,
double-decked pinnaces, and it is difficult to draw a sharp line
between these and frigates.

145

When reefing of the topsail had been introduced it was usual for a small warship, such as a fourth rate, to be rigged without top-gallant masts. It is uncertain when the *studding sail* came into general use, but they are mentioned for the first time in 1549. *Staysails,* which had been used on small boats since the end of the 15th century, were used for the first time on lager vessels

275

about 1660. At about the same time, crowfeet were rigged from the leading edges of the now broad tops to the stay below, to protect the topsail from damage. 1. Studding sail 2. Mizzen staysail 3. Main staysail 4. Maintop staysail 5. Crowfoot 6. Foretop staysail.

276

In 1638 the French had made an early reply to the *Sovereign of the Seas* by building a vessel roughly as large but with only two decks and 72 guns, the *Couronne,* which in a fresh wind could probably fire at least as many deadly broadsides as the heavy English 100-gun ship. Samuel Pepys, then Secretary to the Admiralty, records in his diary that the French built two-decked ships of 70 guns, whose lower deck was 4 feet above the waterline, whereas the English ships, being narrower and more deep-going, had their lower deck only a little over 3 feet above. French three-deckers were about 44 feet wide, the English as a rule not being more than 41. The Frenchmen were better platforms for the artillery and moreover better sailers.

In the "Atlas de Colbert" from 1664—1669 there are, among many other pictures, drawings of a ship of 84 guns with two complete gun decks (276, 277). It has no raised forecastle, and the quarter-deck begins first at the mizzenmast. Its overall length has been calculated to 55 m., length of keel to 39 m., width 13 m., and draught 6 m.

The English three-decker *Prince* (272) of 100 guns had about the same proportions except for the draught which was over 6.5 m. The French ships were built with an eye to fighting the galleys in the wind-impoverished Mediterranean and were therefore strongly armed both fore and aft. In order to have a free arc of fire the beak-head and its rails swept down in a deeper curve than on other ships of the times.

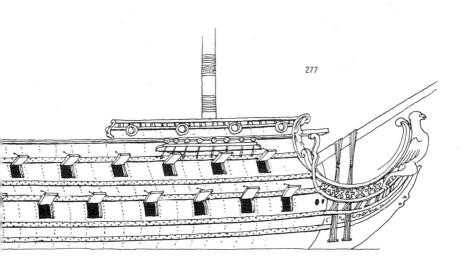

277

Ships in the 18th century

Nor did the 18th century introduce any radical changes. The English rounded stern was adopted by other sea powers, rigs were made more efficient, and the castles became steadily lower. At the beginning of the century the bowsprit was extended with a

jib-boom for the *jib;* the spritsail topmast then disappeared and its sail was set under the jib-boom or dispensed with entirely. The picture (278) shows an English ship of 50 guns of 1773. Soon, too, the part of the mizzen in front of the mast was cut away, so that the sail looked like a gaffsail (279). On smaller ships the long mizzen spar vanished and was replaced with a gaff (280), but large ships retained it for nearly the whole century as a reserve spar should one of the important yards be damaged.

151

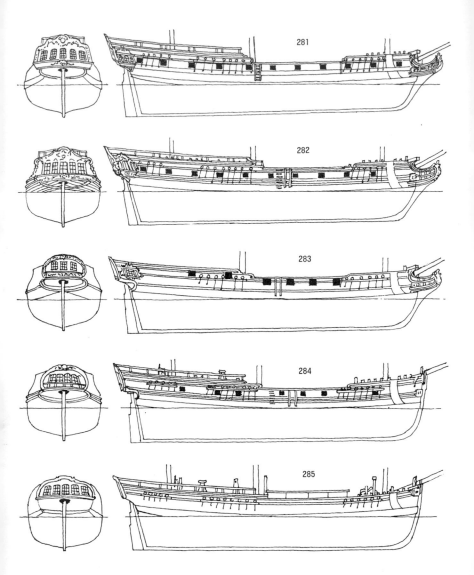

In his work "Architectura Navalis Mercatoria" of 1768 the Swedish master shipwright Fredrik Henrik af Chapman classifies the sea-going merchantmen of Europe. He divides them into five main groups according to details of the hull. A ship the shape of a *frigate* (281) was square-sterned in that the planking came to an end at the *counter* under the decorated upper part of the stern. On a *hagboat* (282) the planking continued up to a beam just under the taffrail. The *pink* (283) seems to have been a development of the Dutch fluyt (273), round-sterned and narrowing above. All these three groups had a beak-head of the same type as contemporary men-of-war. Without a beak-head and therefore much more blunt in the bow were the *cat* (284) and the *barque* (285).

287

286

In 1682 the French introduced a new weapon on a new type of vessel. Mortars had already been used on land for a hundred years, but the first mortar bombardment from sea was suffered by the town of Algiers from French *bomb ketches*. The bomb ketch was quite simply a broad vessel with the foremast removed to make room for the heavy mortars (287). The bomb ketches were more strongly built than ordinary vessels, and sturdy beam bridges supported the deck from below and distributed the shock of recoil when the mortars were fired. The bombs weighed about 200 lbs, which was a great deal when one considers that the balls from the largest guns were of 48 lbs. The bomb ketch (286) is drawn from Chapman's "Architectura Navalis Mercatoria".

153

288

289

290

291

288. A small, two-masted 17th century vessel with square sails on both masts was the *brigantine*. — 289. A Swedish brigantine of 1699 with gaff mainsail and staysail. — 290. Brigantine or *brig* according to Chapman. — 291. *Snow* according to Chapman. The mainmast is full-rigged, and the gaffsail, the *brigsail*, is set on a spar, the "*snow-mast*", aft of the mainmast. Towards the end of the century, when snows and brigs alike carried both fore-and-aft mainsails and brigsails, the name brig became common to both. — 292. U.S. Navy brig from 1810 with royals on both masts. Double upper main studding sails and main topgallant studding sails are set. On the foremast, the fore topgallant studding sail, upper foresail studding sail and lower foresail studding sail.

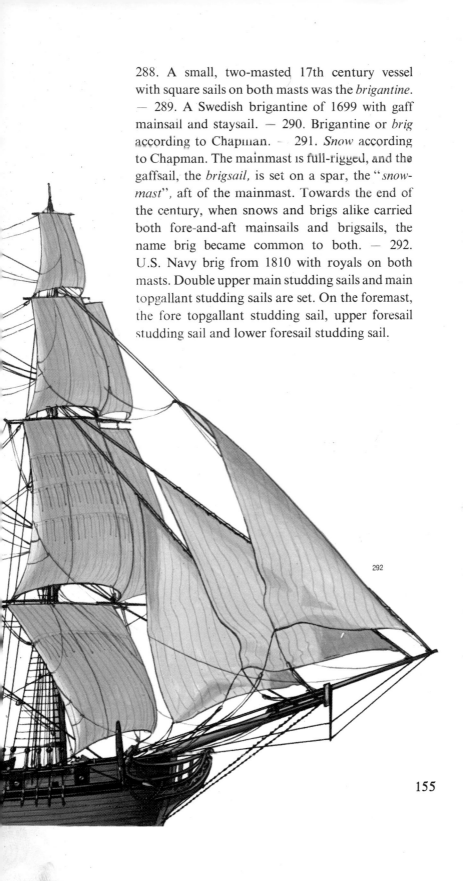

292

293

294

During the 17th century, Dutch inland waters were traversed by a small two-masted pleasure yacht (294) with main and fore gaffs which would today be called a *schooner*. The foremast was later removed and a three-cornered foresail was rigged on a stay between the stem-post and masthead. The gaff-rigged craft was further given a jib on an easily detachable jib-boom and was called a *bezaan jacht* (295).

But slightly larger two-masted yachts seem to have changed in another way. In a drawing from the early 18th century we see a two-masted yacht with a jib-boom and the jib hoisted to the top of the foremast, and this yacht must quite definitely be called a schooner (296).

The gaff-rigged *cutter* which was used in the 18th century above all as a dispatch and patrol vessel seems to have developed in part from the bezaan yacht. An English naval cutter from 1768 (293, after Chapman) carries double *square topsails* and also, on an

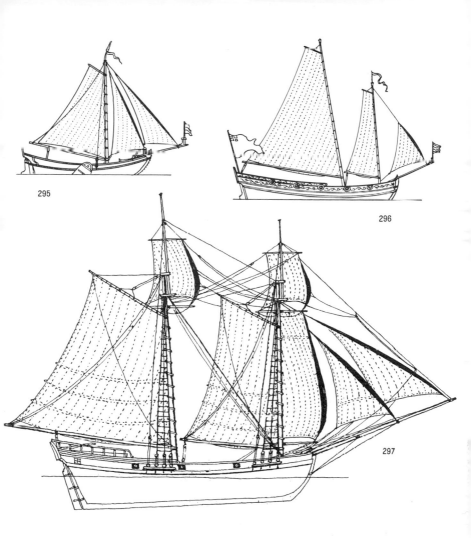

295

296

297

extra yard, a large *running square-sail*. The length of the jib-boom
is four-fifths that of the hull, and at first sight the vessel seems
over-rigged. But the hull is broad and deep-going and would need
plenty of sail in a slight wind. In fresh wind the topmast could be
lowered and the jib-boom drawn in.

By a schooner is understood a two-masted vessel carrying chie-
fly fore-and-aft sail whose after mast is taller than the forward.
Tradition has it that the first schooner was built in Gloucester,
Massachusetts in 1713, but we have seen that the schooner rig
was already in use in Holland during the 17th century. The name
schooner is, however, American. An American schooner from
1760 (296) shows topsails both on the main and foremast and also
a running square-sail with a yard at the foot as well. With a square
sail also under the main topsail the craft could be called a brigantine.

157

298

Little indeed is known of how the *chebeck* originated. The pirates of the Barbary States used the chebeck during the 17th century, and during the 18th century we find both Spanish and French chebecks, towards its end even Russian. It is said that the Spanish built their first chebecks to fight the Algerian pirates with their own weapon.

A model in the Museo Maritimo in Barcelona shows us this elegant and swift craft (298, 300). It is a shallow-draught vessel with concave waterlines in the bows and sides sloping outwards, and the hull has much in common with the galley. It is a light sailing vessel that can attain a decent speed in light winds, and above all is highly manoeuvrable under oars. The Venetian *galeotta* (299) was an oar-propelled vessel with auxiliary sails, and if we think of her as a little broader we almost have a chebeck before

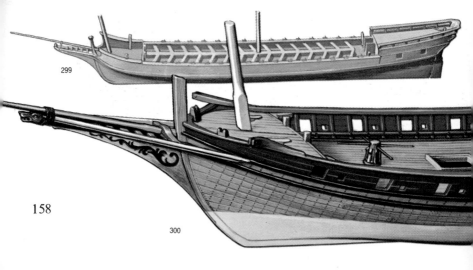

299

300

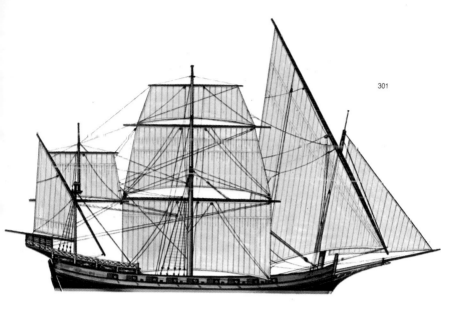

us. But the chebeck was above all a magnificent sailer. Like so many other Mediterranean vessels she had a ram-like beak-head. A "grating deck" projected far out over the round stern as an extension of the quarter-deck.

It is probable that all chebecks were from the beginning rigged with lateen sails on all three masts, but from the mid 18th century we find both Moroccan and French chebecks with mainmasts rigged à la polacca (301). A *polacca* was a square-rigged Mediterranean vessel with the masts in a single piece, without tops, which makes it possible for an upper yard to be lowered close to the lower so that all wind can in this way be taken out of the sail. Towards the end of the century we find also chebecks rigged approximately like ordinary frigates of the time.

159

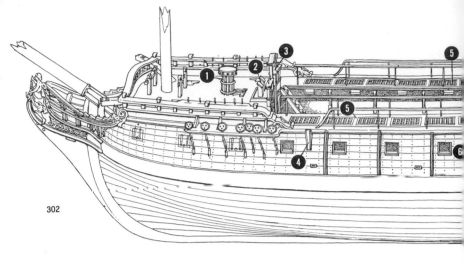

302

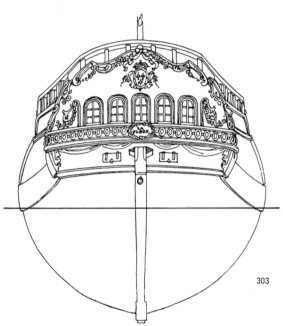

303

The greater part of the 18th century was a period of stagnation for English shipbuilders mainly because of a number of rigid regulations which bound their hands. The result was that both Spanish and French ships came to be larger and better than Englishmen of the same class.

The frigate had gained in importance in nearly all navies. It was built to be a strong, swift vessel for convoy or privateering service. It was well-armed for its size, and during the 18th century the guns were generally mounted on a single deck. The early fri-

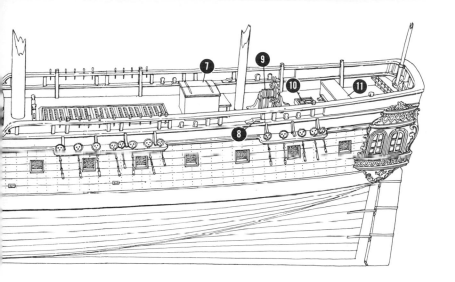

gates usually carried from 24 to 28 guns. By the middle of the century, many were being built which had 32 or even 36 guns, and towards its end there were frigates armed with over 40.

Nearly all French 18th century men-of-war were built with very slightly inclined end-posts, which naturally resulted in concave waterlines near the keel. The frigate *La Flore* was armed with thirty 9-pounders, and her dimensions were: total length 47 m., length of keel 38 m., beam 10.3 m., draught 5 m. The numbers in the picture indicate: 1. Capstan 2. Ventilators for the galley 3. Ship's bell 4. Sheave hole for the main tack (chesstree) 5. Gangboard 6. Sheave hole for the foresheet 7. Casing over the ladder to the gun deck 8. Sheave hole for the main sheet 9. Steering-wheel (The sterring-wheel began to replace the whipstaff at the beginning of the 18th century, but at the middle of the century many ships were still being steered with a whipstaff.) 10. Skylight. 11. Chicken coop.

A class of warship immediately under the frigate was the *sloop,* which was also mainly intended for scouting, convoy and privateer service. These ships were usually rigged as frigates, and carried about 18 guns. They could often be propelled also by oars (304).

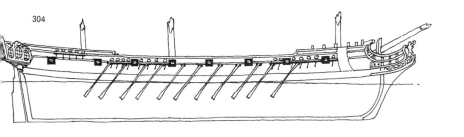

304

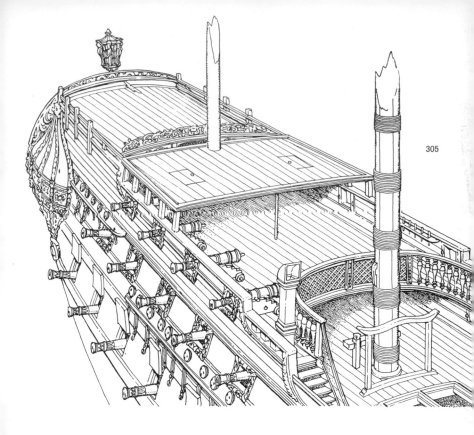

305

Most of the larger merchantmen during the middle and end of the 18th century were rigged more or less like contemporary warships (cf. 278), even if many were still without topgallants and the very largest — or those of the most extrovert shipowners — could carry royals. The large ships of the Dutch East India Company (305, 307) were built, rigged and armed as complete men-of-war, and as loss of life was still great owing to the length of the voyage and bad food a large crew was always taken from home.

On a model of the 54-gun East Indiamen *den Ary* of 1725 (305) we can still see the clinker-laid planks covering the sides of the quarter-deck and half deck, which was to be retained on Dutchmen almost to the end of the century. The quarter-deck is built forward in a sweeping curve around the mainmast, hardly of

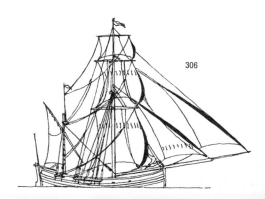

306

307

any use, yet found on most of the Company's large ships. The *sun deck* forward of the poop deck and the half deck ventilator are easier to understand on ships which sailed in the tropics, and these details also became common.

The smaller trading vessels were rigged as snows, brigantines or schooners (cf. 288—297), and the small coastal vessels showed a multifarious collection of sails, from single square sails in the North to different variations of lateen sails in the Mediterranean. Chapman shows for example a *hooker* (306), a *galiot* (308) and a *galeas* (309). Note that this galeas has nothing to do with the galeass, which was a heavy combined rowing and sailing ship, designed primarily for war.

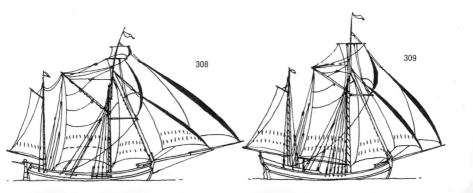

308

309

Warships in the 19th century

Nelson's flagship the *Victory,* now preserved in dry dock at Portsmouth, was already an old ship at the Battle of Trafalgar. She was built during the years 1759—1765, and before Trafalgar was twice

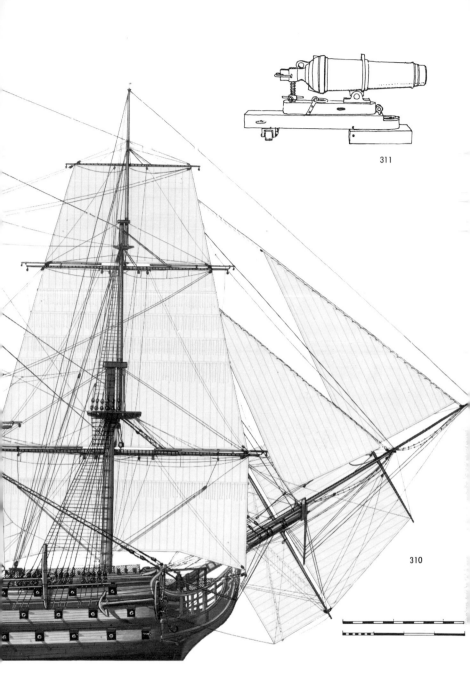

311

310

rebuilt, the open galleries in the stern being covered in and the
channels moved up in line with the forecastle and quarter-decks.
Her spritsail and spritsail topsail were seldom set, but the braces
and lifts of their yards gave the bowsprit and jib-boom good support at the sides. Here, as at Portsmouth today, the *Victory* is
shown as she appeared at the time of the battle.

165

The total length of the *Victory* from the figurehead to the *taffrail* (the uppermost part of the stern) is 69 m., the length of the keel 45.75 m., and greatest width 16 m. Her armament at Trafalgar was: on the lower gun deck thirty 32-pounders, on the middle deck twenty-eight 24-pounders, on the upper deck thirty 12-pounders, on the half deck ten 12-pounders, on the forecastle deck two 12-pounders and two 68-pounder *carronades* (stubby guns for close-quarter work named after the town of Carron in Scotland where they were first made. See 311, previous page).

In the picture of her forepart (312), we see on the farther side the *hammock netting* fitted up on the rail, a row of U-shaped iron prongs and strong netting where the tightly-rolled hammocks of the crew were stowed during the daytime, partly to be out of the way of the guns and partly to serve as protection from shrapnel and light enemy fire. The *bumpkins* for the fore-tacks jut obliquely forwards from the riding bitts on each side of the bowsprit. These became common on English ships in the mid 18th century.

312

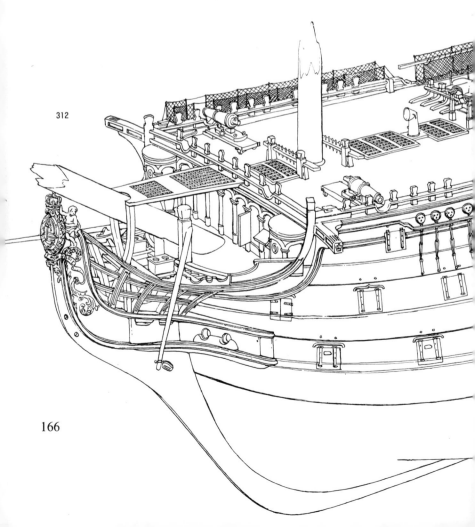

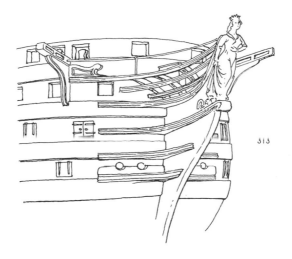

313

Ever since the introduction of the beak-head planking above it had ended in a bulkhead which was weaker than the sides of the vessel. Even at Trafalgar, the upper gun deck still ended in a bulkhead. The stern with its galleries and windows was an even weaker point than the bow, and it was the dream of all commanders to sweep an enemy's decks clean with a raking broadside from astern.

The French and Italians had been building frigates whose planking went right round the bow at the height of the forecastle ever since the 18th century, and after the Napoleonic wars even the larger ships of the line began to be built in this way (313). The stern was also strengthened by being made round, but it was still usually interspersed by large glass doors and windows for the well-being of the officers (314).

314

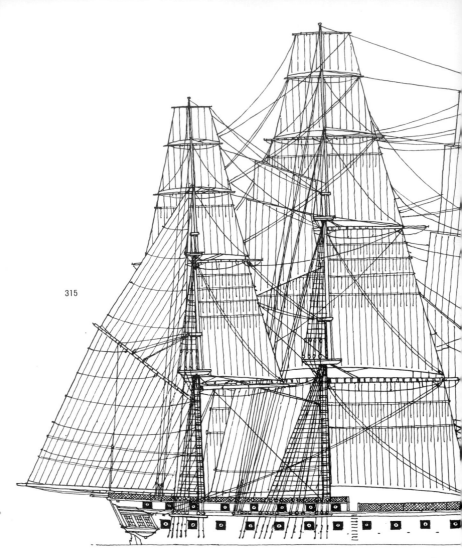

315

The American frigate *President* (315) was launched in 1800, and
with her two sister ships was the largest frigate built to date:
62.2 m. long and 13.5 m. wide. Still larger was the French *La Belle
Poule* built in 1834: 63.7 m. long and 14.7 m. wide (316). She had
the long lines of the frigate, but the mounting of the guns on two

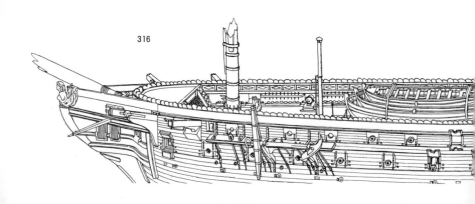

316

The *President* carried thirty 24-pounders on the gun deck, twenty 12-pounders on the forecastle and half deck, and two 24-pounders on the forecastle. She had a fantastic rig with *skysails* on all masts above the royals. We see also a *gaff topsail* above the mizzen.

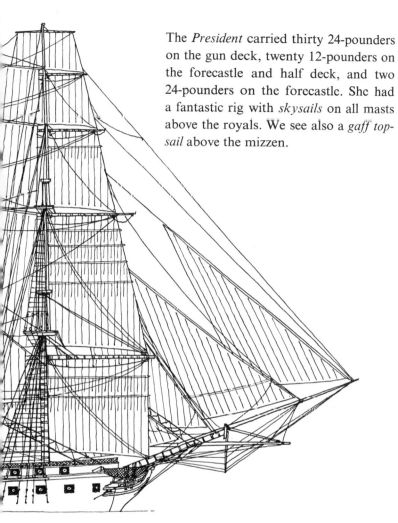

complete decks and their number made her almost as powerful as a third rate ship of the line. On the gun deck she carried twenty-eight 30-pounders, and on the upper deck four 30-pounders and twenty-six 30-pounder carronades. Notice how her beak-head rails have become straight bulwarks.

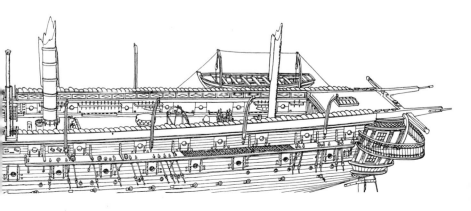

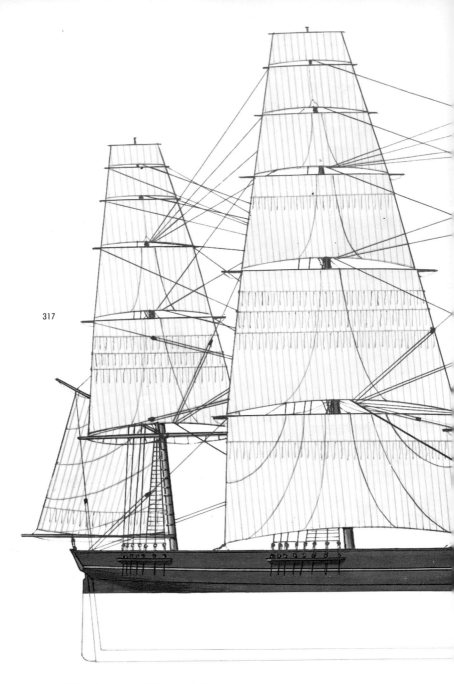

317

The last sailing ships

The *Rainbow* which was launched in New York in 1845 has been described by many as the first *clipper ship,* but it seems to be with clippers as with most other things in seafaring, that they made a gradual appearance as a result of natural development. The so-called *Baltimore clipper* (318), a schooner from the late 18th cen-

318

tury, differed from other small contemporary vessels mainly in its sharp bows, but it probably did not have concave waterlines like the clipper ships to come. The *Rainbow* (317) had slightly concave water lines forward, a deep keel and more speedy lines than later clippers which were swifter because of their great length. She was 47 m. long at the waterline and 9.55 m. broad. Notice the *moonsails* above the skysails.

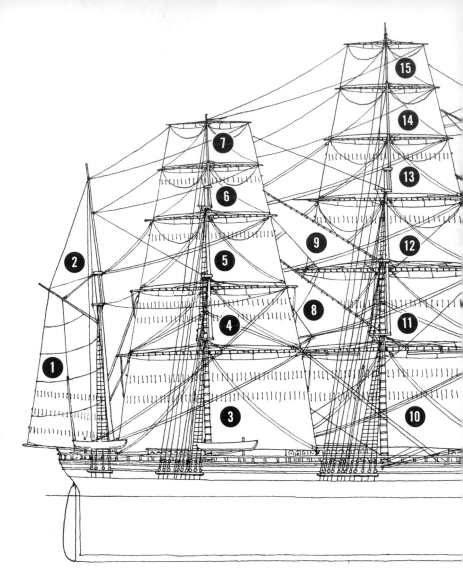

The largest of all clippers and the largest wooden vessel ever to be built was the American *Great Republic,* launched in 1853. She was 99 m. long and 16.2 m. wide, and had four masts which were called, from the bow aft, the foremast, mainmast, mizzenmast and spanker mast. The three first were square-rigged, the last carried a fore-and-aft sail, and today we should call her a four-masted *barque.* To ease manipulation of the rig the topsails were divided into *upper topsails* and *lower topsails.* As she was about to start her maiden voyage a fire broke out on board, and, during the extensive repairs that followed, her hull and rig were cut down so much that she never had the chance of showing what sort of sailer she could have been. She is shown here (319) as she probably looked before the fire. The *Great Republic* sank in a storm

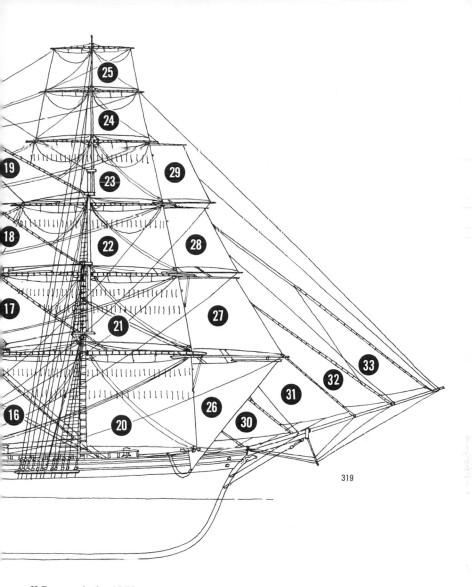

319

off Bermuda in 1872.

The figures denote: 1. Spanker 2. Jigger topsail 3. Mizzen crojack 4. Mizzen lower topsail 5. Mizzen upper topsail 6. Mizzen
topgallant 7. Mizzen royal 8. Mizzen topmast staysail 9. Mizzen
topgallant staysail 10. Mainsail 11. Main lower topsail 12. Main
upper topsail 13. Main topgallant 14. Main royal 15. Main sky-
sail 16. Main staysail 17. Main topmast staysail 18. Main topgallant staysail 19. Main royal staysail 20. Foresail 21. Fore lower
topsail 22. Fore upper topsail 23. Fore topgallant 24. Fore royal
26. Lower studding sail 27. Lower topsail studding sail. 28. Upper
topsail studding sail 29. Upper studding sail 30. Fore staysail 31.
Fore topmast staysail 32. Jib 33. Flying jib.

320

Towards the end of the 19th century all large sailing ships were built of iron and later steel. Even the masts, spars and yards were made of steel tubing, and steel wires and chain replaced a good deal of the hemp lines in the rigging. The bowsprit and jib-boom were made in one piece, and on many vessels the lower mast and topmast were also a single construction. Channels disappeared, and shrouds and stays were made fast with rigging screws.

A *full-rigger* is a ship with at least three masts, all of which are square-rigged. The clipper ship *Rainbow* (317) was a three-masted full-rigger. The German *Preussen* (320) was the only five-masted full-rigger in the world. She was launched in 1902 and was 124 m. long at her waterline and 16.4 m. wide. Like all big sail-propelled vessels from the last days of the sailing-ship she also had double topgallants, the *upper* and *lower topgallants*. With her 47 sails she had a total sail area of 4650 sq.m.

In the picture of the square-rigged mast (321) the numbers indicate: 1. Royal halyard of chain 2. Royal clewline 3. Upper topgallant buntline (The buntlines ran parallel through eyes on the front of the sail as in the picture above, the system being essentially the same as in classical times. Cf. 44, 52, 57 and 63.) 4. Upper topgallant halyard of chain 5. Upper topgallant lifts, which kept the yard under control when it was lowered (cf. 36) 6. Upper topgallant downhaul 7. Upper topgallant foot with buntlines 8. Upper topgallant sheet of chain, which was led in towards the mast and from there to the deck 9. Lower topgallant clewline 10. Lower topgallant sheet 11. Footrope 12. Upper topsail halyard 13. Upper topsail downhaul 14. Lower yard lift 15. Lower topsail clewline 16. Jackstay (In about 1830 a stay, later of iron, began to be fastened along the upper edge of the yard, to which the sails were bent.) 17. Lower sail clewline.

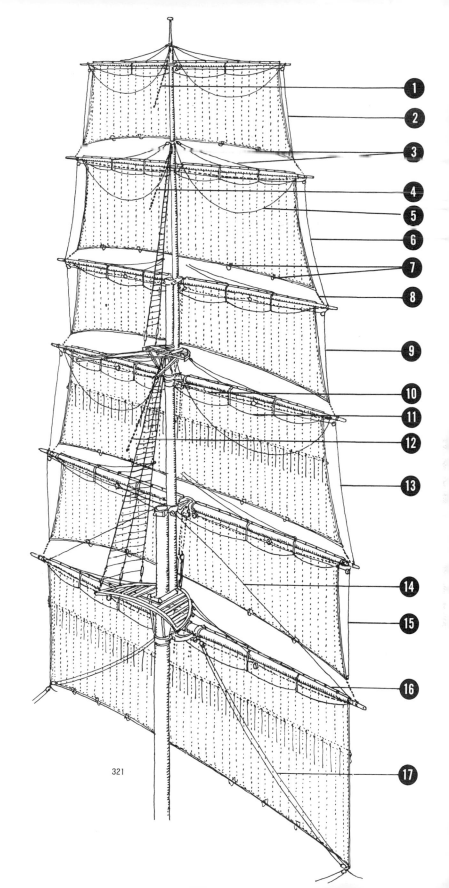

322

323

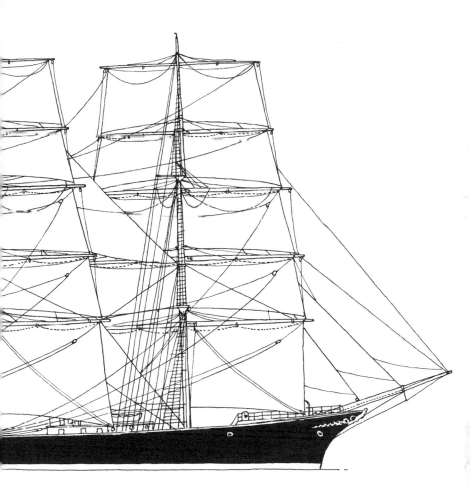

The three-masted barque (323) was the most important vessel in the northern merchant fleets during the nineteenth century. The smaller barques long sailed with undivided topsails and topgallants. On the larger ships, the rigging was simplified as far as possible so that they could be sailed with as small a crew as possible and compete with steamships.

Rigs were cut down, royals and skysails were eliminated, and some ships were built from the start with this simplified rig, an example being the four-masted barque *Pommern* launched in 1903 in Glasgow for a German owner and today a museum in Mariehamn, Finland. Her three square-rigged masts are all of the same length, and yards and sails can be exchanged between masts. The yards are hoisted with steam winches, and the lower yards are checked with brace winches. She is 92 m. long, and 13 m. wide (322).

However, still further simplification was necessary in the attempt to save the sailing-ship.

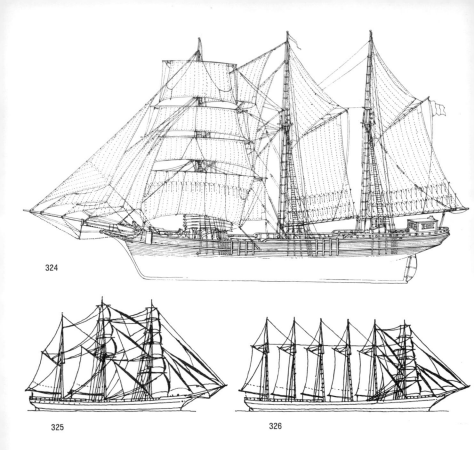

324

325

326

The *barquentine* had not come into existence merely by rerigging the barque, although no more was necessary than that the mainmast was fitted with fore-and-aft sails for the barque to become a schooner-type ship. The French vessels that still fished the Newfoundland banks after the First World War were often rigged as barquentines (324). The masts retained their old names and the only new sail was the *main gaff topsail*.

But it sometimes occurred that a ship was rigged for example with a fore-and-aft sail on the lower mainmast and square sails on the top and topgallant masts (325), and the usual terminology did not then cover the new type. In England all such types of pseudo-barques were called *jackass barques*.

Full-riggers and barques were built in the 20th century only for really long-distance trading and as school ships. In order to make seafaring under sail at all profitable even for coastal work, large barquentines were built which could be manned by a very small crew. Thus emerged the four, five and six-masted barquentines (326).

178

The normal type of *schooner* during the last hundred years of seafaring under sail was a two-masted vessel whose after mast, the mainmast, consisted of lower mast and topmast and carried a gaff mainsail, gaff topsail and staysail. The rig of the foremast varied, and these variations gave different names to the vessel. When the foremast consisted of two parts and carried a gaff on the lower mast and square sail on the topmast, the vessel was called a *topsail schooner* (327). Passing from bow to stern the topsail schooner carried the following sails: flying jib, fore topmast staysail, jib, fore staysail, fore upper topsail, fore lower topsail, foresail, main topmast staysail, main gaff topsail, mainsail. The staysails are fitted with downhauls to facilitate furling. Gaskets hang down from the yards. To protect the mainsail from wear the boom lifts have been given baggywrinkles. The fore staysail is sheeted to a boom.

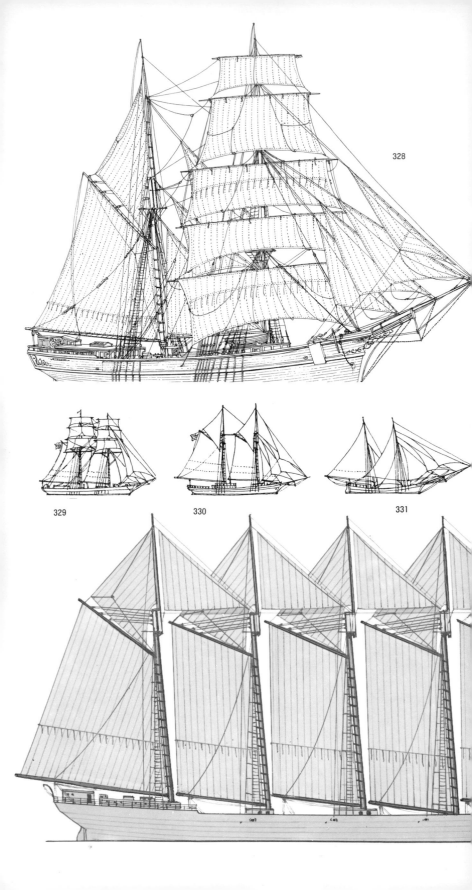

328

329   330   331

002

333

If the entire foremast of a double-masted schooner was square rigged, then the vessel was called simply a schooner, or a *hermaphrodite brig,* and later — somewhat improperly — a *brigantine* (328). There were also schooners with a square topsail on both masts (329), and schooners with no squaresail at all. These were called *fore-and-aft schooners* (330). This type still sails in the Pacific, and in the Mediterranean one can see small schooners with triangular sails (331), almost like modern yachts.

We have already mentioned the ships of schooner type known as *barquentines* (324—326), There were also barquentines rigged with square topsails on one or more masts (332, 333), and large fore-and-aft schooners. The largest of these was the *Thomas W. Lawson* of over 5,000 tons, rigged with seven masts (334). She was 117 m. long, 15.25 m. broad and was manned with a crew of only 16 men. The sails on the five middle masts were identical, and could be easily exchanged.

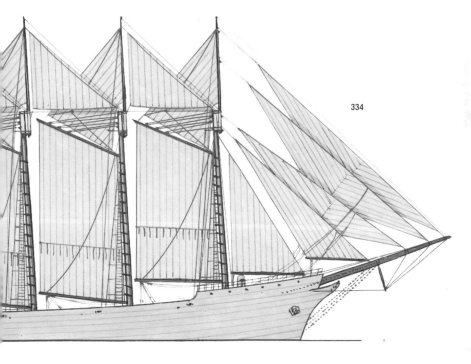

334

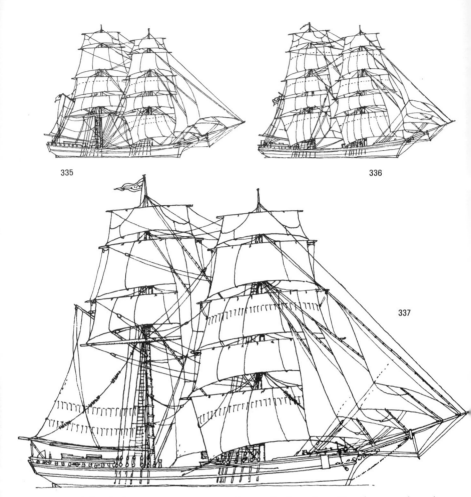

335

336

337

The brig was a two-masted vessel rigged as the fore and main-mast of a barque were with the addition of a large main gaff-sail. About the middle of the 19th century the brig was still common as a small vessel on long ocean routes, but, for the same reason as the full-rigger and barque were rerigged, the brigs proper also began to disappear towards the end of the century. But the snow-brig with brigsail on the "snowmast" aft of the mainmast (335, cf. also 291) was still sailing in this century, and the common brig (336) has long remained as a collier transporting coal from the English mining towns.

The true *brigantine* (337) had no square mainsail. The mainmast often consisted of two parts and always carried a square topsail. When the square topsail on the mainmast was later replaced with a gaff topsail the vessel continued by some to be called a brigantine. Others called it a *hermaphrodite brig* (328).

182   Throughout the 19th century and even after the First World War, the *ketch* (339) was common as a coastal freighter in Eng-

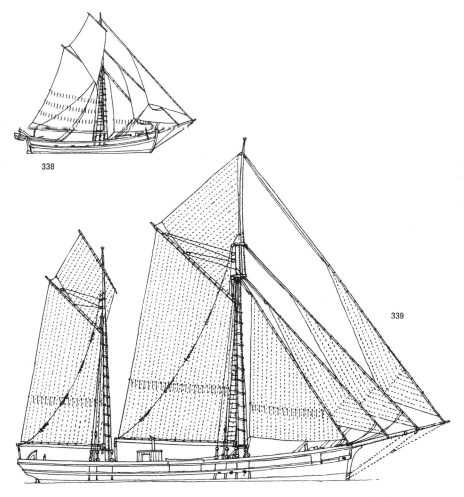

338

339

lish waters. Vessels with the same type of rig, mainmast and miz-zenmast rigged with fore-and-aft sail, continued for many years to sail in Scandinavian waters and were known there as *galeases* (with one s). They are still to be found, perhaps mainly in the Baltic, but they are powered now by engines and can set auxiliary sails on their often shortened masts. The single masted coaster was still common until the Second World War, particularly in Finland. In the picture (338) we see a Danish *jakt*. Freighters of the same type are known in England as *cutters*.

Hundreds of different types of small craft have been sailing in European waters in the past century alone. In some places they are sailing still. This little book contains only the most important vessels, as seen through my eyes. Frequently, I have jumped for-ward many years at a time in my description; I can only hope that this book may still serve as an outline survey of the story of the sailing-ship.

Sources

Åkerlund, H., *Fartygsfynden i den forna hamnen i Kalmar*, Uppsala, 1951.
– *Nydamskeppen*, Göteborg, 1963.
Anderson, R. & R. C., *The Sailing-Ship*, London, 1947.
Anderson, R. C., *Oared Fighting Ships*, Tonbrigde, 1962.
– *Seventeenth Century Rigging*, London, 1955.
– *The Rigging of Ships in the Days of the Spritsail Topmast*, Salem, 1947.
Artiñano, G. de, *La Arquitectura Naval Española*, 1920.
Association des Amis des Musées de la Marine
    La Belle Poule
    Le Chébec
    La Flore
    La Réale de France
Bowness, E., *The Four-Masted Barque*, London, 1955.
Brito, N. de, *Caravelas, Naus e Galés de Portugal*, Oporto.
Brögger & Shetelig, *The Viking Ships*, Oslo, 1953.
Callender, G., *The Portrait of Peter Pett and The Sovereign of the Seas*, Newport, 1930.
Casson, L., *Ships and Boats*, New York, 1964.
– *The Ancient Mariners*, New York, 1959.
Chapelle, H. I., *The Baltimore Clipper*, Hatboro, 1965.
– *The History of American Sailing Ships*, New York, 1936.
– *The History of the American Sailing Navy*, New York, 1949.
Chapman, F. H. af, *Architectura Navalis Mercatoria*, Stockholm, 1768; facsimile, Magdeburg, 1957.
Crone, G. C. E., *Nederlandsche Jachten, Binnenschepen, Visschers-vaartuigen*, Amsterdam, 1926.
Farrere, C., *Histoire de la Marine Française*, Paris, 1956.
Furttenbach, J., *Architectura Navalis*, Ulm, 1629; facsimile, Paris, 1939.
Greenhill, B., *The Merchant Schooners*, I–II, London, 1951.
Halldin, G., et al., *Svenskt skeppsbyggeri*, Malmö, 1963.
Handels- og Söfartsmuseet på Kronborg, *Aarbog*, 1946–1967.
Heinsius, P., *Das Schiff der hansischen Frühzeit*, Weimar, 1956.
Hornborg, E., *Segelsjöfartens historia*, Helsinki, 1948.
Klem, K., *De Danskes Vej*, Copenhagen, 1941.
Konijnenburg, E. van, *Shipbuilding from its Beginning*, I–III, Brussels.
Köster, A., *Das antike Seewesen*, Berlin, 1923.
Laird Clowes, G. S., *Sailing Ships*, I–II, London, 1932.

Laughton, L. G. Carr, *Old Ships, Figure-Heads and Sterns*, London, 1925.

Lindqvist, S., *Gotlands Bildsteine*, Stockholm, 1941.

Lever, D., *The Young Sea Officers Sheet Anchor*, London, 1819; facsimile, New York, 1955.

Longridge, C. N., *The Anatomy of Nelson's Ships*, London, 1955.

– *The "Cutty Sark"*, I–II, London, 1933.

Lubbock, B., *The Blackwall Frigates*, Glasgow, 1924.

– *The China Clippers*, Glasgow, 1946.

Marques, V. de la, *Diccionario de Arquitectura Naval*, (MS), 1719–1759.

Marstrand, V., *Arsenalet i Piraeus og Oldtidens Byggeregler*, Copenhagen, 1922.

Moll, F., *Das Schiff in der bildenden Kunst*, Bonn, 1929.

Monleon, D. R., *Construcciones Navales*, (MS), 1890.

Moore, A., *Last Days of Mast and Sail*, Oxford, 1925.

Morton Nance, R., *Sailing-Ship Models*, London, 1949.

Nour, M. Z., et al., *The Cheops Boats*, I, Cairo, 1960.

Palacio, D. G. de, *Instruccion nautica para Navegar*, Mexico, 1587; facsimile, Madrid, 1944.

Páris, E., *Essai sur la Construction Navale des Peuples Extra-Européens*, Paris.

– *Souvenirs de Marine*, I–VI, Paris, 1882–1908.

Robinson, M. S., *Van de Velde Drawings*, Cambrigde, 1958.

Roërie, G. La, *Navires et Marins*, Paris, 1946.

Ronciére & Clerc-Rampal, *Histoire de la Marine Française*, Paris, 1934.

Rålamb, Å. C., *Skeps Byggerij eller Adelig Öfnings Tionde Tom*, Stockholm, 1691; facsimile, Malmö, 1943.

Salisbury, W. & Anderson, R. C., (ed.), *A Treatise on Shipbuilding and a Treatise on Rigging written about 1620–1625*.

Schoerner, G., *Regalskeppet*, Stockholm, 1964.

Sjöhistorisk Årsbok, 1943–1966.

Stenton, F., *The Bayeux Tapestry*, London, 1957.

Stevens, J. R., *Old Time Ships*, Toronto, 1949.

Svenska Flottans Historia, I–III, Malmö, 1942–1945.

Svensson, S., et al., *Nautiskt bildlexikon*, Göteborg, 1963.

The Mariner's Mirror, 1–54, 1911–1968.

Torr, C., *Ancient Ships*, Chicago, 1964.

Ucelli, G., *Le Navi di Nemi*, Rome, 1950.

Underhill, H. A., *Deep-Water Sail*, Glasgow, 1952.

– *Sailing Ship Rigs and Rigging*, Glasgow, 1938.

Warrington Smyth, H., *Mast and Sail in Europe and Asia*, London, 1929.

Winter, H., *Der holländische Zweidecker von 1660/1670*, Leipzig, 1967.

– *Die katalanische nao von 1450*, Magdeburg, 1956.

Museums

Altona, Altonaer Museum
Amsterdam, Nederlandsch Historisch Scheepvaart Museum
Antwerp, Nationaal Scheepvaartmuseum
Barcelona, Museo Maritimo
Boston, Museum of Fine Arts
Cairo, Egyptian Museum
Copenhagen, Ny Carlsberg Glyptotek
Greenwich, National Maritime Museum
Genoa, Museo Navale
Göteborg, Sjöfartsmuseet
Hamburg, Museum für Hamburgische Geschichte
Helsingör, Handels og Söfartsmuseet, Kronborg
Lisbon, Museu de Marinha
London, British Museum
　　　　Science Museum
Madrid, Museo Naval
Mariehamn, Sjöfartsmuseet
New York, The Metropolitan Museum of Art
Oslo, Norsk Sjöfartsmuseum
　　　Vikingskipshuset
Paris, Musée de Marine
Rotterdam, Maritiem Museum Prins Hendrik
Stockholm, Statens Sjöhistoriska Museum
　　　　Vasavarvet
Venice, Museo Storico Navale

Index

187

Permission to Play

How Teens Can Build a Life
That is Fun, Fulfilling, and Promising

by

Joe Fingerhut

Stonebrook Publishing
Saint Louis, Missouri